JS
309
T4

30409 -2

Teaford, Jon C.

The municipal revolution
in America

Date Due

 Printed In U.S.A.

The Municipal
Revolution
in America

The Municipal Revolution in America

Origins
of Modern
Urban
Government
1650-1825

Jon C. Teaford

The University of Chicago Press
Chicago and London

Jon C. Teaford received his B.A. in 1969 from Ober-
lin College, his M.A. and Ph.D. (1970 and 1973)
from the University of Wisconsin at Madison. He is
now an assistant professor of history at Iowa State
University. This is his first book.

The University of Chicago Press, Chicago 60637
The University of Chicago Press, Ltd., London

Library of Congress Cataloging in Publication Data

Teaford, Jon C
    The municipal revolution in America.

    Bibliography: p.
    Includes index.
    1. Municipal government—United States—History.
I. Title.
JS309.T4   352'.008'0973   74–33512
. ISBN 0–226–79165–3

Contents

Preface

Between the early seventeenth century and the early nineteenth century Western man experienced an upheaval in his social, economic, and intellectual environment great enough to shatter the framework of his habits, customs and beliefs. During this age, labor-saving machinery gradually supplanted the handicrafts of the past, while emerging industrialism fattened the purses of merchants and manufacturers. More effective use of the land and an improved quality of livestock limited the age-old danger of famine and upgraded most people's diets. Advances in scientific and medical knowledge eliminated the scourge of smallpox and encouraged unprecedented efforts to rid man of other forms of pestilence. And the writings of John Locke, Thomas Jefferson, and Adam Smith introduced ideas of individual liberty and self-determination to a public familiar only with the strictures of mercantilism and the rigid authority of despotic monarchs. In 1630 the divine right of kings, the bubonic plague, and the hand loom were very real parts of life. By 1830 each had either disappeared or was fast disappearing, a victim of the changing currents of knowledge, intellect, and technology.

Amid this climate of change, men in both Britain and America sought to adjust their institutions of urban government to the fresh realities of human existence. In 1600 urban rule rested in the hands of those admitted to the commerce of the city, and this limited body of commercial participants expected the municipal corporation to devote the largest portion of its time and effort to regulating and promoting trade. Such a government, however, could not survive in a world infected by the philosophy of a Thomas Jefferson or an Adam Smith. Nor could it maintain its barriers to enterprise in an era bursting with the pressures of nascent industrialism, booming commercial development, and soaring urban populations. Instead, this model of municipal government had to succumb to the forces of change and adapt to the nineteenth-century world.

This book narrates the story of this adaptation, describing the transformation in the political structure, function, and external relationships of the American municipality between 1650 and 1825, the vital years in which Americans discarded the model of urban government inherited from medieval Europe and substituted an ideal which determined the course of municipal development up to the present. This change occurred not in a single city, or in a single nation, or on a single continent, but throughout the Western world. Thus the following account will not focus on the local politics or local history of an individual city and will not emphasize the social or political environment peculiar to one urban area. Instead, it will identify the forces molding the municipal corporation as an institution within Western life and avoid preoccupation with local political wrangling. Local politics in Philadelphia or New York City may have influenced how or when the transformation occurred there, but the vital changes identified in this study also took place in such faraway cities as London and Liverpool.

In dealing with this subject of municipal development, I have been able to draw upon the works of others who have studied urban life in early America. For example, Carl Bridenbaugh's *Cities in the Wilderness* traces the development of municipal services during the first half of the eighteenth century but attributes that evolution not to a change in priorities but to the exigencies of population growth and urbanization. Ernest Griffith's *History of American City Government: The Colonial Period* is a work from the 1930s dealing with urban government before 1776, and Judith Diamondstone's doctoral dissertation on the Philadelphia corporation presents a highly useful description of one of the most important municipalities. Yet no previous work has described the vital transformation during the decades from 1725 to 1825, a period of prime significance in the history of urban rule. This study will attempt to fill the gap left by earlier scholars.

Numerous people have helped me in preparing this history of America's municipal antecedents. Professor Stanley Kutler of the University of Wisconsin was indispensable in guiding the project, and professors Stanley Schultz, James Willard Hurst, and Stanley Katz also offered many useful suggestions. Professor Samuel Daykin of Ohio State University was most helpful in affording me the use of library facilities, and Gail Momirov assumed the painstaking task of typing the manuscript. Of special aid was my mother, Virginia Teaford, who offered her perceptive comments on the early drafts of this work. And special thanks also go to my father, Robert Teaford, who financed me during the years spent on this project and provided invaluable assistance in its preparation.

I also thank the *American Journal of Legal History* for permission to reprint portions of chapter 6 which appeared in the January 1973 issue.

1   The
     Commercial
     Community

1   The
English
Background

When the first English settlers reached North America, they carried with them the customs, traditions, and institutions of European civilization. Their cultural baggage was the product of centuries of evolution and development, a complex mass bearing the mark of many peoples and places. Yet it was not only an inheritance from the past but a legacy for the future; for Europe's laws, habits, and institutions continued to guide the course of life in the New World. These instruments of social organization would determine the development of America's schools, churches, homes, and markets. They would serve as a base for colonial existence and as a foundation upon which the colonists would build a new nation.

Among the traditions transported to the New World was the institution of the municipal corporation. By the Elizabethan age hundreds of cities and boroughs interrupted the green expanse of England's countryside, and governing each was a municipal corporation adapted to the needs of a trading and industrial community. Centuries of urban existence had molded this form of local rule, and English colonists did not readily abandon these time-honored governmental practices. Rather, the idea of the municipal corporation crossed the Atlantic and set the parameters for city life in urban centers flanking the Hudson, the Delaware, and the James. The English municipality was the preface to urban history in the New World—the starting point from which the saga of the Amercian city began.

Essential to understanding this European background is a recognition of the municipality's unique role as a center of trade and commerce. Amid the agricultural world of medieval Europe, cities existed as alien bodies requiring extraordinary powers and special protection. Feudal ties adapted to the land-oriented society of lord, vassal, and serf were not suitable to the producers and traders whose livelihood depended on manufacturing and commercial mobility. These townspeople were participants in a commercial rather than a subsistence economy and as such required a relative freedom from the manifold trade barriers and tax burdens imposed by rural nobility. Moreover, a trading community demanded rules of commercial conduct, standards of price and measure, and quality controls on manufactures, all subjects beyond the understanding of the lord of the manor or the knight of the shire. Thus the wants and needs of the city were not those of the vast majority of the people who tilled the land and harvested the crops. Instead, town life represented a special case, an anomaly demanding anomalous institutions.

The municipal corporation developed as the chief of those anomalous institutions. English kings from the Normans through the Stuarts granted charters of incorporation drafted to serve the needs and peculiarities of communities of butchers, tailors, merchants, and drapers. Commerce was the organizing principle of the municipality's government, and its offices, suffrage requirements, ordinances, and pageantry all reflected the economic practicalities underlying its existence. The municipal corporation was a community of trade and industry, an organization molded by the distinctive needs of commercial life amid a world of subsistence agriculture.

The municipality's structure of political participation reflected this commercial focus. In the typical borough of Tudor-Stuart England, only those eligible to engage in commerce possessed any political privileges. The body of borough freemen enjoyed both the exclusive right to trade within the community and the sole privilege of participating in its government. If one were not a freeman and could not trade, one could claim no role in the corporation's politics. For the municipal corporation was a commercial community in which the commercial class was the governing class.

The requirements for admission to the rank of freeman also mirrored the economic peculiarities of an urban existence. By 1600 the municipal corporation generally awarded freeman status only to children of freemen, persons apprenticed in a trade, or those who paid an admission fee. Thus whereas a political voice in rural Britain rested on landholding, in the boroughs this privilege depended on the commercial property of vocational skill or hard cash. With the exception of two of England's more than two

hundred municipalities, freeholding was not a requisite for municipal office or the franchise in city elections.[1] Instead these privileges
were dependent on proof of a vested interest in the commercial
community either through birth, participation as a craftsman, or
money investment.[2]

Moreover, nonresidents as well as residents could claim such a
stake. Almost one-third of the freemen of Liverpool during the
reign of James I traded within the city and voted in municipal
elections but lived outside the corporation limits. No matter
whether they resided in the nearby towns of Roby and Wavertree
or in the very heart of the borough, as participants in the commerce
of Liverpool they were citizens of the municipality with the full
rights of corporate membership.[3]

In some boroughs trade interests even underlay the apportionment of municipal council seats. Thus Elizabethan York disregarded geographic wards and apportioned its thirty-eight common
councillors among twenty-six different occupational groups.[4] Similarly, in the borough of Morpeth each of the seven vocational
companies held permanent claim to one seat on the board of
aldermen.[5] Commerce, and not residency, defined participation in
these municipalities, and accordingly representation conformed to
occupational and not geographic divisions.

The actual role of Tudor-Stuart freemen in governing such
commercial communities varied considerably among England's
numerous municipal corporations. London's freemen filled vacan-
cies on the life-tenure board of aldermen and annually elected the
common council but left the choice of lord mayor to a combination
of aldermen and senior guild members.[6] Freemen in England's
second largest city, Norwich, exercised similar voting rights,
choosing a legislative body of twenty-four lifetime aldermen and
sixty short-term councillors as well as annually nominating two
mayoral candidates from whom the aldermen selected the municipality's chief executive.[7] In the smaller borough of Berwick-upon-
Tweed, however, the freeman's participation in municipal government reached its greatest extreme; for in this Northumberland
corporation those admitted to the commerce of the borough
gathered in common assembly to elect all officers, instruct them as
to their duties, and personally enact each ordinance.[8] In such a
municipality the ideal of a self-governing body of artisans and
merchants neared realization.

Yet in many English boroughs the freemen's political role declined markedly during the Tudor-Stuart period. Although there was no change in London, Norwich, or Berwick, in most of Britain's cities power fell into the hands of a life-tenure body of aldermen and councillors. The borough citizenry exercised no voice in the election of these officials. Rather, when one of the board or council seats became vacant, the remaining members would themselves choose a replacement from the body of freemen. Freeman status did generally entitle one to a voice in selecting the borough's representative to Parliament, and it also was prerequisite for entry into the corporation's self-elected government. But beyond this it carried few political privileges. As early as 1512, the officials of Nottingham warned that if the electorate were allowed "to rule and follow their appetite and desire, farewell all good order."[9] Others seemed to agree, and by 1700 the rule of approximately two-thirds of England's municipalities lay in the hands of self-perpetuating oligarchies.[10]

Yet the ruling officials of the closed corporation were not members of a narrow, aristocratic clique but were citizens drawn from a wide range of modest trades and occupations. During the first quarter of the seventeenth century, the borough sheriff of Nottingham was most frequently a moonlighting butcher or tanner, not a lordly despot as in the tales of Robin Hood. Fishmongers, vinters, coopers, glovers, and apothecaries also found an opportunity to serve in this position, as did representatives of fifteen other trades.[11] Similarly, during the twenty-five-year period from 1557 through 1582, the self-elected councillors and mayors of Oxford included men of at least eighteen occupations ranging from painter and skinner to barber and tailor. Thomas Perry, "gentleman," served on the Oxford city council along with William Fumes the baker and William Ward the innkeeper.[12] In Oxford as in Nottingham, municipal government rested in the hands of ordinary traders and craftsmen, and no matter the mode of election these men were the ones who were determining the course of urban rule in Britain.

These municipal leaders may have represented a variety of occupations, but they focused their lawmaking efforts on one area. Ordinances, orders, by-laws, and minutes all reveal that the chief concern of city government was to regulate and promote commerce. The borough's business, like its political structure, centered on the requirements and demands of an urban life of trade and manufacturing, and preeminent among these demands were the control of commercial behavior and the stimulation of economic activity. Fair trading, a just division of wealth, and future prosperity were vital to the harmony and survival of the urban community, and it was the responsibility of the municipal corporation to ensure such equity and welfare.

The regulatory function was especially significant in molding the activities of the municipal corporation. Englishmen of the preindustrial age viewed their nation's economy as an economy of scarcity, a fragile system where the waste of excessive competition and the knavery of inequitable dealing could mean poverty and famine for thousands. They consequently believed that economic survival depended on precise rules of commercial conduct and the strict allocation of vocational duties and opportunities. Townspeople feared unfair competition, shortages, and malapportioned economic power. They had seen "the poor . . . pinch for hunger and . . . children . . . cry in the streets not knowing where to have bread" because certain covetous souls had supposedly sought "immoderate gain by enhancing the price of corn."[13] To prevent such widespread suffering, Englishmen expected government to intervene and limit the rapacity of heartless individuals. Government bore responsibility for protecting the poor from the rich, the small operator from the large, and the native producer from the foreign.

As a vital element of government, the municipal corporation was duty-bound to enact those market rules and vocational codes necessary to ensure economic justice and prosperity. It was England's urban magistrates who were to guard the community against economic rape by the greedy. Through its ordinances and by-laws the municipality endeavored to protect producers from cutthroat competition and consumers from faulty commodities and shoddy workmanship. The pessimistic mind of the Tudor-Stuart age was not willing to leave the division of England's limited wealth to the hand of nature or the supposed laws of economics. Rather, Englishmen relied on the hand of the alderman and the laws of the municipal corporation for the just apportionment of goods and money.

The municipality's first step in allocating commercial resources was to restrict entry into the various trades and crafts. To practice as an artisan or engage in trade within a municipal corporation, one first needed to become a freeman, a status granted at the discretion of the mayor and aldermen. By exercising this discretion the corporation could limit the number pursuing a vocation and ensure each producer enough business to remain solvent. Thus the Nottingham corporation repeatedly prosecuted nonfreemen who practiced weaving, brewing, barbering, or tailoring "to the great wrong and abuse" of the municipality's trade and industry.[14] Similarly, in the borough of Reading cobblers, clothdrawers, and collar-makers all deplored "the great hurt and damage" caused by outside craftsmen and encouraged the corporation to exclude a total of 26 such interlopers during the decade 1623 through 1632.[15] This figure was insignificant, however, when compared with Liverpool's list of 184 presentments issued against nonfree traders during the reign of James I.[16] Of top priority to the city fathers of Liverpool, Reading, and Nottingham were the economic interests of the borough citizenry, and consequently aldermen and councillors did not hesitate to punish dangerous usurpers of the freemen's trading monopoly.

Borough officials, moreover, excluded not only undesirable manufactures and sellers but also unwanted purchasers of scarce raw materials. For example, in 1555 the borough of Stratford-upon-Avon bolstered the local candle trade by ordering the town's butchers to sell their tallow only to fellow townsmen and not to outside traders.[17] Likewise, in 1566 Northampton's council attempted to ensure a ready supply of leather for the city's glove and shoe industries by ordaining that no stranger shall "come into this market . . . to buy any hide or hides . . . but that he or they shall bring in quantity as much leather ready tanned into this market to sell."[18] And twenty years later the same borough protected its store of vital cereals by forbidding nonfree maltsters to purchase any barley in the city market unless they offered for sale an equal quantity of another grain.[19] Merchants and manufacturers needed raw materials, and such ordinances as these were meant to ensure that each received his share.

In a further attempt to guard vocational rights, the borough required each craftsman to work solely within the bounds of his own occupation. As early as 1534 the councillors of Oxford acted against those who by engaging in more than one craft contributed to an inequitable society of a "few rich or thrifty men and great multitude of poor and needy." To correct this wrong, the city fathers restricted brewers, bakers, fishmongers, butchers, vintners, and chandlers to "only one of the foresaid victualling occupations by itself without dealing or meddling with any of the other."[20] In like manner the borough of Beverley forbade innkeepers to make bread for anyone but their immediate families, while Stratford-upon-Avon flatly ordered that "none do bake bread to sell within the borough but only the common bakers appointed for the same."[21] The city of York applied a similar rule to tailors, forbidding them to assume the skinner's duty of furring gowns, collars, or cuffs.[22] And in 1622 the cobblers of Reading presented a petition "against the shoemakers for mending of old shoes once worn" contrary to the borough ordinance restricting manufacture to shoemakers and repair to cobblers.[23] Brewers were to brew, skinners to fur, and bakers to bake, and it was the responsibility of the municipal corporation to preserve this harmonious division of duties.

The corporation's regulatory hand, moreover, not only calmed the fears of competitive producers but also guarded the interests of vulnerable consumers. Throughout the Tudor-Stuart age, England's boroughs sought to establish rules that would ensure an abundant supply of quality goods and services at a reasonable price. Their consistent aim was to punish the shyster and slipshod artisan while aiding the honest purchaser. As a beneficent mediator the municipality stood ever ready to intervene among bargainers and adjust the scales of the marketplace to the scales of justice.

In order to make this adjustment, the English borough established standards of weights and measures and fixed the price of common necessities such as bread and beer.[24] Leicester, Oxford, and Stratford-upon-Avon also set the price of tallow, while Beverley's council determined the changing cost of oatmeal and London's aldermen fixed the rate for coal.[25] Wage levels for laborers and porters were subject to the will of York's municipal corporation, as were the fees charged by the city's skinners.[26] Thus in boroughs throughout Britain the uncertainties of marketplace haggling did not determine the price of vital commodities. Instead this duty rested in the corporate hands of the borough government.

Other municipal regulations were aimed not at fixing prices but at barring private traders from doing so through the practice of forestalling. Those seeking to forestall trade would purchase commodities en route to market with the intent of reselling at a higher price. To prevent this and to guarantee an equal opportunity to bid on produce, the Beverley corporation outlawed the purchase of oats before they arrived at market, and the city of London forbade fuel dealers to intercept ships carrying coal from the Newcastle upon Tyne region.[27] Similarly, the borough of Liverpool repeatedly presented traders "for buying butter before it come to market only to sell it again," and the assembly of Great Yarmouth ordained that none "shall take or buy any butter coming or brought toward or to this town . . . but in the market place."[28]

Related to forestalling was the practice of engrossing. Engrossing entailed purchasing a large segment of the available supply of a commodity in order to raise its price above normal market level. Between 1603 and 1625 Liverpool's corporation found this monopolistic practice especially troublesome and issued a total of sixty-eight presentments for engrossing such varied products as grain, fruit, butter, eggs, hemp, and tallow.[29] The aldermen of Northampton faced a similar problem with bakers who bought "every market day great number of grain to their own lucre and advantage and to the raising of the price of grain."[30] Likewise the city of York strictly limited the quantity of cereal that hawkers and other middlemen could purchase.[31] In each of these instances, the city fathers would not permit a fortunate few to tilt the balance of commercial power. Rather, buyer and seller were to stand as equals, with the weaker party bolstered by the authority of the municipal corporation.

Safeguards against shoddy merchandise were almost as numerous as ordinances fixing prices and protecting the market mechanism. For example, the borough of Beverley levied heavy fines on oatmeal dealers for selling meal which was "fire fanged" or made of "mowburnt oats" as well as punishing carpenters for offering wares fashioned from "sappy" or unseasoned wood.[32] York likewise penalized skinners who "sell old furs for new" and ordered locksmiths "that no lock be made . . . of dross nor of andiron but of good iron and meet for such work."[33] Further, the borough of Newcastle under Lyme forbade "butchers to sell any victual . . . which is corrupt, fulsome or unwholesome for man's body," and Leicester only allowed the sale of beer which was "good and wholesome for man's body and not red, ropy nor raw."[34]

To enforce these quality restrictions as well as the cost and market regulations, the municipal corporation appointed officers responsible for testing, gauging, and pricing. Leicester's officials included three testers of fish, three of meat, and five of leather, and

two ale tasters per ward.[35] In Saint Albans enforcement of commercial ordinances rested in the hands of the corporation's leather
sealers, viewers of the market, and flesh and fish tasters.[36] Other
cities employed cloth searchers, wool weighers, herring packers,
and a variety of miscellaneous officers capable of surveying the
chief industries of the community.

But the municipal corporation was not merely a negative force
restricting and regulating commerce. It also performed numerous
positive functions intended to stimulate the pace of commercial
activity throughout the kingdom. By building trade facilities and
organizing commercial events, boroughs from Berwick in the north
to Penzance in the south provided economic incentives vital to the
prosperity of Britain and necessary to the country's future growth.

The municipal corporation performed this promotive function
through a variety of policies and programs. First, the great
majority of England's boroughs operated public markets as centers
of trade for both urban dwellers and agricultural producers. De-
pending on the size of the city and the diversity of its commerce,
the corporation might maintain many specialized marketplaces,
including one specifically devoted to wool, one for leather, one for
meat, and one for fish. Most municipalities also held annual fairs
varying in length from three days in Newcastle under Lyme to
fifteen in Kingston upon Hull to forty in Great Yarmouth.[37] At the
time of these fairs, the corporation suspended all the usual restrictions on entry into the community, allowing freeman and outsider
alike to practice their crafts and sell their goods. Further, the
English boroughs often constructed and maintained such vital
commercial facilities as docks, ferries, warehouses, and livestock
pounds, and some even owned grist and fulling mills for the use of
local producers.[38]

Many municipal corporations supplemented these promotive
efforts by engaging in schemes to assist young artisans and
struggling industries. Thus sixteenth-century York operated a
combination school and workshop instructing persons in spinning
and weaving, with the hope of both relieving unemployment and
reviving the city's faltering cloth industry.[39] During the 1620s the
borough of Reading attempted to achieve this same end by loaning
various clothiers cash sums ranging from twenty-five to two
hundred pounds.[40] Moreover, in an effort to gain vital technical
information for the troubled clothing industry, the Reading corpo-

ration sent two of its councillors on a journey "into the West country to view the manner of making their white cloth."[41] Through such travels and aids, the city fathers vigorously sought to bolster the economic base of the commercial community and to further the growth of manufacturing and trade.

But questions of trade and manufacturing did not absorb all the time and talent of the Tudor-Stuart corporation. Numerous problems bearing no direct relation to commerce also appear in the municipal records, testifying to the varied concerns of the aldermen and councillors. Thus in some communities the borough government authorized or encouraged such public works as street paving, lighting, and water conduits and confronted the public safety questions of health, night watch, and fire prevention. In the cities of York and Reading poor relief was a significant subject of municipal concern even though the Elizabethan poor laws had placed questions of indigence primarily in the hands of churchwardens and parish overseers rather than municipal corporations. Moreover, charitable bequests enabled a number of boroughs to administer tuition-free grammar schools vital to the education of such promising urban offspring as William Shakespeare.

Admitting the existence of these activities, one must still recognize their secondary importance compared with the municipality's raison d'etre, commerce. This is evident from the Book of Common Minutes for the city of York, a volume recording the corporation's business with the exception of judicial proceedings. In these minutes for the years 1570 through 1588 one finds 114 entries focusing on trades and markets, 53 relating to poor relief, 19 dealing with such public works as bridges, streets, lighting, and waterworks, and a mere 8 referring to health and safety.[42] The Great Order Book of Beverley likewise includes all the extensive ordinances and shorter orders of a more formal and permanent nature enacted by the aldermen and councillors of that borough. Of the laws listed for 1596 through 1670, 2 short orders deal with questions of poor relief, 1 with public works, 6 with public safety, and 16 with issues of trade, while all 16 of the lengthy, detailed ordinances focus on the regulation of specific vocations and crafts.[43]

When the mayor and aldermen sat in their judicial capacity as municipal court, they again found trade regulation the chief subject of controversy. Of the prosecutions before the municipal magistrates of Liverpool during the decade 1605 through 1614, violations of the freeman's commercial monopoly ranked first in number with a total of 65. Holding second place was the class of violent crimes known as "tussling" or "fraying," numbering 55, followed closely by 49 prosecutions for the market offenses of engrossing and forestalling.[44] The minutes of Norwich's Court of Mayoralty reveal a similar pattern, with inquests into the craft of worsted weaving producing a total of 271 penalties during the period 1630–32, far ahead of the second most frequent judicial business, the 118 prosecutions for vagrancy, begging, wandering, and idleness.[45] A wide variety of crimes and controversies arising under common law, parliamentary statute, and municipal ordinance appeared before the courts of Liverpool and Norwich, but dominating the docket of both cities were questions of commerce and manufacturing.

The duties of the corporations' officers also reflect this commercial preeminence. By 1625 the municipal corporation of Liverpool annually chose thirteen officials dedicated solely to governing the city market and enforcing trade restrictions. Yet only two of the borough's officers devoted themselves primarily to suppressing physical violence and theft, while four assumed the duties of street cleaning. And there were no municipal health officers or any borough officials chosen to oversee the work of poor relief or fire protection. The officers of the municipal corporation were not single-minded in their endeavors, but there was little doubt as to the focus of their attention.[46]

This commercial preoccupation so evident in the legislation, adjudication, and executive functions of the borough further appears as a dominant factor in the field of municipal financing. Whereas agricultural economies have often based their taxation on real property or polls, England's municipalities instead relied primarily on trade exactions in the form of import or sales duties, licensing fees, or rents from commercial facilities. Generally city fathers turned to direct taxation in the form of a property or poll assessment only to finance an occasional public work or pay an extraordinary expense. Otherwise taxation was indirect and closely linked to the commercial functions of the borough.

One of the chief sources of borough revenue was the rent from such corporation properties as markets and docks. Butcher stalls, produce stands, fair booths, and wharfage were all much in demand and thus were valuable assets to the municipal government. The borough of Reading rented out everything from oatmeal stalls to sheep pens, and the city of Great Yarmouth exacted from each fishing boat using its extensive harbor facilities a portion of that boat's herring yield.[47] Similarly, Northampton leased shop space in its town hall, and Liverpool's corporation-owned warehouses proved a lucrative source of revenue for that growing port city.[48]

Corporations also wrenched income from retailers and manufacturers by charging for the privilege to work, trade, import, and sell. Dues charged for admission to the status of freeman and fees for the licensing of innkeepers and victuallers both added much-needed revenue to city coffers. Of additional aid were the tolls exacted from traders transporting goods into the borough. Nottingham levied taxes on imported malt, the borough of High Wycombe earned much revenue from a toll on all grain brought to its town market,[49] and duties on water freight played a major role in financing the port cities of Liverpool and Gloucester throughout the first half of the seventeenth century.[50]

Many of England's municipalities also earned revenue from properties not directly linked to efforts at commercial regulation or promotion. Thus the borough of Winchester during the Elizabethan period was landlord to a lucrative collection of 115 houses and cottages.[51] Northampton's holdings were not so great but did include 32 residences, a scattered acreage of meadowland, and assorted small gardens and orchards containing a total of 64 apple trees.[52] Some boroughs such as Leeds and Norwich, however, owned virtually no noncommercial property, and consequently they continued to squeeze an income from traditional trade exactions and the charitable gifts of wealthy townspeople.

Each municipality's authority to tax, legislate, and adjudicate, however, depended in large measure on the degree of autonomy granted by the borough charter. These royal patents defined the powers and jurisdiction of the municipality by fixing the governmental boundaries separating borough, county, and crown. Throughout the medieval period the commercial community had consistently sought to redefine these limits so as to eliminate the external control which rural lords and magistrates exercised over urban producers. Traders and manufacturers desired a system of self-government adapted to their economic interests, not a life of subjugation to powerful landlords or royal appointees. Autonomy was their goal, and gradually they achieved it.

Many features of the municipal charters reflect this desire for freedom from external authority. Thus one common charter provision granted borough freemen exemption from the myriad of local tolls levied throughout Britain. In 1589 the city of Leicester obtained partial freedom from the royal charges levied against its trade, but as late as 1600 the town fathers were struggling to eliminate the burdensome dues exacted by the Duchy of Lancaster.[53] Other boroughs such as Bristol, Coventry, Norwich, and Nottingham were fortunate enough to acquire county status, a position which exempted them from the interference of rural magistrates. These municipalities elected their own sheriffs, exercised the full jurisdictional authority of a county, and owed no fealty to officials of the surrounding shire.

At the close of the seventeenth century, the municipal corporation eliminated still another source of outside interference by clearly establishing its privileged status relative to both crown and Parliament. During the 1680s Charles II and James II had embarked on an autocratic campaign to harness municipal authority through the forfeiture and surrender of borough charters. The Glorious Revolution, however, put an end to such royal efforts and established the municipal corporation as an inviolate segment of the British constitution. Theoretically Parliament might still limit or alter municipal powers without the consent of the municipality, but the prevailing attitude of the times ensured that in this case the theoretical would never resemble the real. For Englishmen of the late seventeenth century viewed any encroachment by the central authorities upon borough privilege as a tyrannical violation of vested rights and an insult to the hallowed principles of 1688. Expressing the sentiment of the period, one pamphleteer wrote, "To destroy Charters would be in effect to destroy England."[54] And no one in Westminster proposed the destruction of either.

Thus by 1700 the municipal corporation had achieved a protected status within the framework of British government. Once the crown had granted the corporation of London or Norwich a body of powers, neither king nor Commons would dare to violate this grant. Privileges which the crown had bestowed could not be retrieved without arousing the libertarian anxieties of every Engglishman.

2   The Commercial
     Community
     in America

Twice weekly the town crier of colonial Albany,
New York City, or Philadelphia would sound his bell to signal the
start of business in the municipal corporation's market. Among the
corporation-owned stalls strolled corporation officials employing
corporation standards of weights and measures to gauge the
produce sold by corporation-licensed butchers and corporation-
admitted freemen. Elsewhere in the marketplace were cereals,
hides, and cordwood which had traveled by corporation-owned
ferry to corporation docks and had there passed the scrutiny of
corporation viewers and corders, only to be carried away by
corporation-appointed porters working at rates fixed by the corporation. At every step in the transport, sale, and purchase of
commodities the colonial municipality intervened, performing the
vital role of promoter and regulator. For before the 1730s and 1740s
the American borough, like its British ancestor, was primarily a
commercial community governed by commercial participants for
the service of trade and industry. Merchants and artisans had
carried this European concept of urban government to the new
continent, and during the first century of English colonization it
molded the nature of the American municipality.

The settlements which would inherit this governmental tradition
were as yet barely worthy of the name city. In 1700 America's
centers of trade and industry were not sprawling metropolises but
tiny outposts serving the sparsely settled farmlands of the Atlantic
seaboard. The "city" of Albany consisted of a few paths serving as
streets and had fewer than one thousand citizens. Downriver in
New York City, the number of inhabitants had passed four
thousand, but the area of urban settlement had not expanded
beyond the southern tip of Manhattan Island. Philadelphia
had existed for only two decades and could claim only a few
thousand residents clustered along a short stretch of the Delaware

River. Each of America's commercial centers was a compact settlement in which residents could easily walk from one side of town to the other. On the whole, the principal centers of colonial trade and commerce were tight little communities ranging in population from a few hundred to a few thousand, and as yet none could hope to rival Norwich or Edinburgh, let alone London or Paris.

These little towns along the Atlantic coast were united by a common excuse for existence. Each served as a trade depot through which the goods of the surrounding countryside exited and imports from abroad entered. They were the chief points of distribution within the colonies, the focus of all buying, selling, bartering, and trading. Moreover, they were also the hub of the manufacturing crafts—the home of the shoemaker, tinsmith, chandler, and baker. In these settlements the artisan practiced his trade and the merchant bought, sold, and shipped his goods. Although small in size, they were great in commercial importance.

It was due to both the desire for commercial regulation and the need for developing commercial potential that many of these towns sought and received charters of incorporation. For example, William Penn granted the Philadelphia charter of 1691 in order to achieve "the more immediate and entire Government of the said Town and the better Regulation of Trade therein," and in 1701 he established the corporation of Chester "for the better encouragement of settlers and regulations of trade."[1] Similarly, in 1720 George I, through Governor William Keith, incorporated the borough of Bristol, Pennsylvania, with an intent "to promote trade, industry, rule and good order amongst all our loving subjects"; and in 1730 the royal governor of New Jersey included these same words in the preamble to New Brunswick's charter.[2] The Annapolis patent of 1708 emphasized the commercial possibilities of the Maryland port, describing it as a "commodious place for trade" and "the chief mart of the whole country."[3] Likewise Perth Amboy's charter of 1718 explained that city's incorporation by citing its admirable location as "a place of trade" and its "harbor for shipping preferable to those in the provinces adjoining."[4] By 1750 fourteen such chartered corporations lined the Atlantic seaboard from Albany in the north to Norfolk in the south, each created as an instrument for stimulating commercial development by regulating and promoting trade.[5]

In the years following incorporation America's aldermen and councillors fulfilled the expectations of their royal and proprietary benefactors, devoting the bulk of their legislative effort to promoting economic order and growth. An analysis of the compiled ordinances of New York City for 1707 reveals that 54 percent of the content centered on enforcement of equitable dealing, allocation of vocational privileges, and supervision of commercial facilities, while the remainder dealt with such annoyances as street obstructions and untethered animals, the safety measures of fire and crime prevention, such public works as paving, and miscellaneous provisions governing behavior on the Sabbath (see table 1).[6] An examination of Albany's ordinances enacted during the period 1710 through 1724 discloses a similar pattern, with 60 percent focusing on the promotion and regulation of trade while a scattering of enactments dealt with the danger of drunken Indians and the nuisances of wandering livestock and lumber blocking the roadway.[7] Only the titles of Philadelphia's ordinances survive for the years 1705 through 1724, but of the thirty-four measures drafted during this period, again more than half concern commerce, with the minority confronting such subjects as the night watch, street repair, galloping horses, and "mischief arising from dogs."[8]

TABLE 1   Content Distribution of
City Ordinances, 1705–24

Content	New York City 1707	Albany 1710–24	Philadelphia 1705–24
Trade	54.0%	59.9%	52.9%
Annoyance	11.6%	6.5%	8.8%
Public Safety and Order	8.0%	11.0%	11.8%
Public Works	2.1%	8.8%	17.6%
Administration	7.0%	2.2%	2.9%
Other	17.3%	11.5%	5.9%

Thus while Albany was but a frontier stockade with miry paths substituting for streets and a set of leather buckets for fire protection, the city's leaders were building extensive fur depots and drafting detailed ordinances governing what, where, and how traders should barter for the valuable pelts of the Iroquois. Likewise, New Yorkers trod dusty thoroughfares along open sewers to draw putrid water from the city well at the same time that the municipal corporation was constructing wharfs, cranes, jetties, and market houses for the use of shippers and dealers. No mention of street paving appears in the borough minutes of Lancaster, Pennsylvania, until 1774; yet from 1742 onward this same municipality organized two commercial fairs each year as well as semiweekly markets serving both urban and rural producers. New Brunswick's municipal government played no part in educating the young, but it did devote time and talent to constructing an impressive market house and a large pound for penning animals brought to the borough for sale.[9] Fairs, markets, pounds, and docks were all primary concerns of the municipal corporation, outweighing secondary questions of safety, comfort, learning, and religion. In America as in Europe the municipal corporation tackled a wide range of problems, but a preoccupation with commerce persisted throughout the first half of the eighteenth century.

Illustrative of this continuity is the persistence of the freeman status. The charters of Albany, New York City, New Brunswick, and Elizabeth each granted to those admitted as freeman the sole right to "use or exercise any art, trade, mystery or manual occupation," and during the seventeenth and early eighteenth centuries these cities showed little reluctance in enforcing this trade monopoly.[10] Between 1686 and 1724 Albany enacted seven ordinances aimed at preserving the privileges of the corporation's freemen, and in 1701 the common council ordered sixteen interlopers to "be discharged from using their trade or handicraft within this City."[11] In 1691 New York City's council ordered the townspeople "to produce their Freedoms to Retail or use any handicraft trade" and empowered Councilman Thomas Clarke to examine these certificates of freedom and fine any violators.[12] Thousands of New Yorkers were to obtain this privilege during the colonial period, with 582 gaining admission to the freeman class between 1694 and 1706.[13] As late as 1738 the New Brunswick corporation demonstrated its dedication to English tradition by ordering two of the borough's journeymen to purchase the freeman's privilege or face prosecution.[14]

Philadelphia's corporation also tried to restrict commercial status. In 1705 the common council drafted an ordinance forbidding nonfree dealers from keeping shop or practicing as master craftsmen, and six years later it limited the leasing of market stalls to those who enjoyed the freedom of the city.[15] The municipal fathers launched a vigorous attempt to establish the freeman status in 1717, and the council devoted six weekly meetings solely to the granting of freedoms. By the close of this six-week period the corporation had admitted 424 additional traders and artisans to the privileged status.[16] During the following year, Philadelphia's magistrates continued to enforce exclusionary ordinances and imposed the extreme penalty of imprisonment on an offender who was illegally pursuing the butcher's trade.[17]

Municipal magistrates, however, were not rigid in their devotion to the freeman's monopoly, and New York City's aldermen willingly provided certain nonfree women with a special license to trade. Thus in 1704 they granted a mariner's widow the "Liberty to follow any Lawful Trade or Employment within this Corporation for the better Obtaining a livelihood for her and her family."[18] This had become a regular practice by 1708 when they bestowed upon the Widow Robinson the "Liberty to follow any Lawful Trade . . . in such a manner as the Widows of freemen of this City do hold and Enjoy."[19] When faced with widows or other unfortunates, the municipal fathers did not adhere inflexibly to the freeman's monopoly. They could bend and make exceptions, but they did not extend an automatic welcome to anyone who might intrude upon the commerce of the community.

This same fear of open, unrestricted competition is seen in a number of other measures. For example, Albany's by-laws of 1686 guaranteed the prosperity of the city's transporters by ordering "that there be five Carmen and no more appointed . . . by the Mayor and Court of Aldermen."[20] In like manner, the city fathers of seventeenth-century New York ruled "that there be Twenty Carmen And no more" as well as restricting the number of butchers to those licensed by the municipality.[21] Moreover, in 1676 the city froze the number of tanners at two and ordained that only one man might practice as currier within the corporation limits.[22] By the eighteenth century New York's aldermen and councillors were also offering protection to established shopkeepers by outlawing the business of street sellers and peddlers.[23] Similarly, the burgesses of Lancaster, Pennsylvania, sought to preserve "the Rights and Privileges of the Shopkeepers and Trading Part" of their borough by prohibiting "travelling Chapman" from erecting stalls for the sale of goods.[24] The leaders of Lancaster, New York, and Albany all adhered to the Old World belief that unregulated vocational opportunity would ultimately end in commercial impoverishment. Thus they looked to the municipal corporation to limit the number of sellers, transporters, and manufacturers and thereby guarantee each a profit.

Albany's charter of 1686 imposed an even more significant restriction on vocational opportunity by granting that city and its inhabitants a monopoly on fur trading within the province. The charter limited fur trading to Albany's freemen, and these dealers could barter with Indian trappers only inside the city stockade.[25] Anyone who was not a freeman or who sought to practice fur trading beyond the stockade walls would suffer prosecution. For example, in 1686 the mayor's court confiscated "234 gilders in strung wampum, nine pair of Indian stockings, and eight deer skins" which Rene Poupar had acquired in violation of Albany's monopoly, and it also fined the guilty party a sum of forty shillings.[26] In 1707 the conscientious city sheriff brought charges against a prominent trader and former alderman John Lansing, who supposedly "did . . . apply himself & Spoke to an Indian with a pack without the Stockades of this said City."[27] Moreover, the sheriff and his deputies did not hesitate to raid the homes of suspected malefactors in nearby Schenectady and search for evidence of illicit trading with the Indians. In 1719 Albany's officials seized from a Schenectady residence "two pieces of Strowd" used for bartering with the Indians, and they conducted a similar raid on the village in 1721.[28] Despite bitter complaints from the people of Schenectady, Albany's city fathers were determined to maintain those restrictions on vocational opportunity which were specified in the municipal ordinances and charter.

Albany's corporation went one step further in apportioning vocational opportunity and proceeded to battle the dangers of economic concentration. As early as 1678 traders had complained that twenty to thirty persons in Albany were monopolizing commerce with the Iroquois.[29] To check such concentration and secure "a more equal distribution of the Indian Trade among the Inhabitants of this City," the city fathers in 1686 declared that "no Trader who hereafter shall sell Duffells, Strouds, Blankets" or other large goods shall also offer such small wares as "Knives, Looking Glasses, Painting stuff, Boxes . . . Bells, Thimbles, Beads, Indian Combs and Needles." By thus dividing the trade, the municipal corporation ensured that those "whose mean stock renders them incapable of dealing in Commodities of greater value" would at least have an opportunity for bartering bells, beads, and thimbles free from the crushing competition of more prosperous operators. Albany's aldermen also attempted to bolster the competitive position of those smaller dealers who had no overseas ties by forbidding traders to purchase their trinkets and tools directly from Europe or the West Indies. Consequently, dealers with special suppliers or London agents were not to possess an advantage over those less fortunate, but all were to compete on an equal basis.[30]

Municipal regulation of pricing sought in a similar manner to even the score between powerful traders and vulnerable customers. To prevent an inequitable balance among bargainers, the charters of Chester and Bristol bestowed upon these boroughs the authority to determine prices for "bread, wine, beer, wood, and other things."[31] During the seventeenth and eighteenth centuries, New York, New Brunswick, Philadelphia, Lancaster, Burlington, New Jersey, and Wilmington, Delaware, all fixed the cost of bread, while Albany's council set the rate for both bread and beer.[32] Albany, New York City, and Philadelphia likewise established the fees charged by carters, and New York determined ferrymen's tolls.[33] Borough leaders in Pennsylvania and New Jersey, like those in Lancashire and Kent, thus rejected the unregulated market as a mechanism for allotting essential goods and services and instead placed this allocative function in the hands of the municipal corporation.

Though municipal officials had the authority to fix these rates, the actual prices often depended not simply on the aldermen's judgment but also on the expectations and demands of the regulated artisans. Thus as early as the Dutch period in New York's history, city leaders readjusted bread prices in response to the complaints and threats of angry bakers. In 1659, for example, New York City's bakers went on strike and refused to bake until the municipal fathers increased the rate on bread. In that year, and in 1661 and 1663 as well, they succeeded in winning some concessions, and bakers met with equal success in both Albany and New York City in the years following the English conquest.[34]

The carters were less successful in their attempts to influence the fixing of municipal price schedules. In 1677 the carters of New York City went on strike and gained nothing from their efforts except a fine of three shillings apiece.[35] Seven years later in 1684 fifteen carmen again went on strike and refused "to Obey, Observe and follow the Laws and Orders" established by the city council for the regulation of their trade. In response the municipal fathers ordered the strikers "Discharged from being Any longer Carmen" and proclaimed that "all and Every person ... within this City have hereby free Liberty and License to Serve for hire or Wages as Carmen (The said Carmen now discharged, and Slaves Excepted)." Confronted by this action three of the striking carters confessed their wrongdoing, paid a fine of six shillings, and agreed to adhere to the municipal regulations. The city council then admitted these three to a reconstituted corps of municipally licensed carters, but the twelve remaining strikers seem to have permanently lost their right to transport goods within the city.[36] In 1695 the carmen again petitioned for a raise in their rate schedule, and the council again defied the transporters and refused their request.[37] Thus the relationship between the regulator and the regulated differed from trade to trade. While bakers were often able to gain some concessions from the magistrates, the carters of the seventeenth century wielded no such influence over the fixing of prices or the general government of their trade.

At the same time that colonial aldermen were struggling to restrict the incomes of bakers and carmen, they also were endeavoring to limit marketplace profiteering through ordinances aimed at the practices of forestalling and engrossing. Thus in 1684 the city of New York ruled that "no Person Shall Forestall Any Provisions or Victuals Coming to the Market" or "Engross any Provisions or Victuals which is in the Market."[38] In Albany the aldermen legislated against those who "for their own private lucre and gain ... engrossed the fur trade," forbidding such men to intercept Indian trappers en route to the city.[39] Likewise, New Brunswick ordained that "no person shall buy ... any provision going to Market," while Annapolis resolved that "none of the inhabitants of this city shall buy any flesh or fish, living or dead, eggs, butter, or cheese" except in the corporation marketplace.[40] Lancaster also suffered from "the market being forestalled ... by some particular persons in order to retail at an advanced price" and penalized such sharp dealers with a fine of twenty shillings or a sentence of three to ten days in the workhouse.[41]

When certain necessities were in extremely short supply, the municipal corporation became especially concerned about the engrossing of goods to the detriment of the general public. During the "Bread Famine" of 1696 Albany's common council observed that "several people do go with money in their hands to buy wheat and cannot have it" because the merchants had engrossed the grain supplies, "being resolved to ship it for New York." To remedy this situation and foil the merchants' scheme, the Albany council resolved that "no merchant or any other person . . . shall ship any corn aboard any sloop, vessel, boat whatsoever."[42] Through such emergency action the city fathers of Albany sought to prevent suffering and starvation and limit the dire effects of economic greed.

In still another effort to protect marketplace bargainers, the colonial corporations pursued a thorough program of standardizing and inspecting weights and measures. Seventeenth-century New York appointed a grain measurer to ensure fair dealing in the sale of wheat, corn, barley, and rye, as well as "inspectors of white and brown bread" to inquire "if the bread be of proper weight and quality."[43] In the early eighteenth century the city fathers also enacted ordinances to ensure that "all Butter exposed to Sale . . . have the Quantity of Weight the same contains marked thereon" and that all retail sales of beer or cider conformed to a "Wine Measure duly sealed According to Law."[44] During this same period the corporation of Philadelphia employed officials for "ascertaining the Dimensions of Casks" and "the Cording & Measuring of fire Wood."[45] And in 1744 the borough of Lancaster enacted an ordinance penalizing those selling cords of three-foot length rather than the standardized English measure of four feet.[46] In a community dependent on commerce for its livelihood, a gallon in the market had to equal a gallon at the dock, and this week's cord had to equal last week's. Standardization was essential, and in America as in Britain the municipal corporation sought to guarantee such uniformity.

And not only did the municipal corporation control competition, regulate pricing, and outlaw faulty measures, it also attacked shoddy commodities and craftmanship. The city of Albany chose "two or more fit persons yearly" to judge whether grain offered for sale within the corporation was "good and merchantable."[47] New Brunswick required that "no unwholesome or Stale Victuals be sold in the market," and New York City annually appointed four gaugers, packers, and cullers to mark all casks of beef or pork "as

Shall be good and wholesome Meat fit for Transportation."[48] Describing local artisans as "seldom Masters of their Trades," New York's aldermen and councillors in 1711 sought to upgrade craftsmanship by extending the required length of the apprentice's indenture from four years to seven.[49] Whereas during the period 1694 to 1707 only 37 percent of the city's indentures were for a term of seven years or more, after the reform of 1711 95 percent of the indentures were for this time.[50] Similarly, the city of Philadelphia hoped to discourage artisans "not Qualify'd to Exercise their Trades" by allowing guild companies of "Manufactors . . . to be incorporated the better to Serve the Public."[51] From Albany to Norfolk, the colonial municipalities each endeavored to eliminate the foul and slipshod, thereby guaranteeing a high standard of goods and services to the urban consumer.

Thus, in America as in Britain questions of quality, quantity, price, and vocation were all subjects of municipal concern. The artisans and merchants of Albany, New York, and Philadelphia had clung to an Old World concept of urban rule and applied it to the New World environment. Though the business of Albany's corporation focused on Indians and furs and that of Leicester or Reading on weavers and cloth, the basic goals of aldermen in frontier New York and urban England remained identical. Each sought to apportion vocational opportunity, guarantee equitable dealing, and maintain commercial facilities with the hope of ensuring present solvency and future prosperity.

The men who drafted America's ordinances and by-laws were well qualified to deal with questions of urban commerce, for the colonial aldermen and councillors were drawn from an extensive variety of commercial interests. America's cities were primarily hubs of mercantile endeavor, and in New York City between 1675 and 1725 64 percent of the council members for whom occupational data is available earned their living as merchants. Another 31 percent were artisans and innkeepers, and the remaining 5 percent worked as schoolteachers, lawyers, or farmers.[52] There was a similar distribution of occupations among those serving in Philadelphia's city government from 1701 to 1726. Sixty-seven percent of Philadelphia's aldermen and councillors were merchants, 26 percent pursued trades, and 7 percent primarily earned their income as lawyers.[53] Merchants dominated the government of these mercantile centers, but a large number of artisans also served on city councils and spoke for the manufacturing interests of urban America.

Moreover, these numerous tradesmen represented a wide variety of manufacturing crafts. The sixteen artisans who served as members of Philadelphia's corporation from 1701 to 1726 represented fifteen different crafts, and New York's council also included masters of fifteen trades. In 1701 the first city council of Philadelphia could claim among its members a tailor, a ship captain, a brewer, a carpenter, a shopkeeper, and the operator of a fishery as well as four merchants.[54] And during this same year in New York City, six merchants served on the city council, together with a flour bolter, a silversmith, a builder, and a pumpmaker.[55] Many of those classed as merchants also engaged in manufacturing as a lucrative sideline. Councilman Henry Badcock of Philadelphia was a brewer as well as a merchant, and his colleague Nehemiah Allen was also a cooper.

No matter what their trade, these municipal leaders were generally successful businessmen who had individually proved their ability in commerce. Municipal officials like Edward Shippen and Anthony Morris of Philadelphia not only ranked among the most prosperous merchants in the city but also were large landowners and real estate speculators.[56] Peter Schuyler, the first mayor of Albany, built the foundations of the Schuyler family fortune through shrewd fur trading, and his prosperous relatives and descendants served in the government of both New York City and Albany for decades.[57] The first chief burgess or mayor of Chester, Pennsylvania, Jasper Yeates, was also a man of considerable means who lived in a handsome brick mansion and owned a mill, a granary, and a bakery in the vicinity of the borough.[58] In Philadelphia, Albany, and Chester, the municipal corporation was not exclusively a rich man's club, but a disproportionate number of the leaders bore financially prestigious names.

The same was true of the municipal fathers of New York City. While New York City taxpayers in 1697 held an average of 54 pounds worth of property, the estates of those serving as mayor, recorder, councilman, and alderman from 1695 to 1700 averaged 145 pounds.[59] Alderman and mayor Nicholas de Meyer maintained extensive trading operations, owned a farm in Harlem, and also held property in England and the Netherlands.[60] Mayor Cornelius Steenwyck lived in an impressive house with velvet chairs trimmed in silver lace, alabaster figurines, marble tables, and tapestried cushions.[61] Not all municipal leaders, however, were so fortunate. Of the eighty-three persons listed in the tax rolls for the Out Ward of New York City, thirty-eight possessed more property than the ward's two councilmen, Thomas Turneur and Peter Oblimis, both of whose estates were valued at only 25 pounds.[62]

Leaders such as Shippen, Schuyler, Meyer, and Steenwyck not only made and executed municipal law but also served as municipal judges. In the majority of America's cities and boroughs, the mayor and aldermen presided over a local court which enforced municipal ordinances and mediated a variety of other disputes. For example, the cities of Albany and New York both enjoyed county status and had the power to hear all civil causes, with no appeal from decisions involving sums of twenty pounds or less. Further, these same municipalities possessed the authority to prosecute "all manner of petty larcenies, riots, routs, oppressions, extortions, and all other trespasses and offences" committed within the corporation limits.[63] The mayor and aldermen of Elizabeth enjoyed "full power and authority to enquire of, hear and determine" a similar list of crimes, and Philadelphia's magistrates judged "treasons, murders, manslaughters, ... felonies and other offences, capital and criminal."[64] The charter of Annapolis limited the civil jurisdiction of that city's court to suits involving sums not exceeding six pounds, ten shillings, and the aldermen of Williamsburg and Norfolk could hear only civil cases in which the amount at stake was twenty pounds or less.[65]

By mediating common-law contract disputes, these municipal courts extended the corporation's commercial role far beyond that embodied in the city ordinances. Debtor-creditor suits, controversies involving damage to freight, struggles between master and apprentice, employer and employee, buyer and seller, all filled the mayor's court docket in New York and Philadelphia. For example, in 1670 the mayor's court of New York City settled a dispute between the city's shoemakers and the city's two tanners, who "neglect to grind or pound their tan, according to agreement entered into and made between them."[66] In another case New York's magistrates heard a woman complain that her employee "is behaving very stubbornly ... and will not attend to his work," while the employee replied that "he cannot remain in the house because the plaintiff always raves and scolds so."[67] In these disputes and innumerable others, the mayor and aldermen served a vital role as mediator. As judges as well as legislators, the municipal magistrates focused much effort and attention on the need to ensure harmony and fair dealing between supplier and purchaser, worker and master.

America's municipalities also furthered the regulation of commerce by enforcing parliamentary and provincial trade laws. New York City's municipal magistrates heard a larger percentage of cases arising under the English trade and navigation acts than any other common-law court in the province.[68] Those who transported goods directly from continental Europe rather than by way of Britain would find themselves standing before the mayor's court bench, as would those who sought to break the English monopoly on trade with the colonies. Just as the city ordinances attempted to allocate the commerce of Manhattan among urban dwellers, so the mayor's court upheld the effort of Parliament to govern and promote the wealth of the empire.

Commerce also underlay the financing of the various municipalities lining America's Atlantic seaboard. Each of these cities wrested income from butchers and vendors by leasing market stalls, and rents from fair booths provided a borough such as Lancaster with approximately two-thirds of its income.[69] Likewise, Annapolis enjoyed the right to levy "reasonable toll upon such goods, cattle, merchandizes, and other commodities as shall be sold" at the city fairs. Williamsburg fixed a similar toll, and Norfolk exacted four pence for each load of beef brought to market, three pence for each lamb, and two pence for every hog.[70] New York earned the bulk of its revenue from rental of corporation-owned ferries and docks, and Philadelphia enacted a wharfage tax of one shilling for every ton loaded and unloaded at the city docks.[71]

Fees for admission to the commercial status of freeman were another source of municipal income. In seventeenth-century New York, one acquired freeman status only through apprenticeship or through purchase, which cost artisans one pound, four shillings and merchants three pounds, twelve shillings.[72] Translated into goods, the craftsman's fee equaled the cost of approximately two hundred pounds of bread, or a year's supply for two persons, and the trader's amounted to six hundred pounds of bread, or enough to support six persons for twelve months. Albany's merchants also paid three pounds, twelve shillings for freeman status, and the city's craftsmen purchased the privilege for one pound, sixteen shillings, a sum equal to the cost of three hundred pounds of bread.[73] Added together, such fees represented a small but welcome asset to the municipal corporation, constituting approximately 3 percent of New York City's revenue during the typical year 1691–92[74].

Even more profitable were the noncommercial properties held by New York and Albany. By charter grant both these municipalities received "all the waste, vacant, unpatented, and unappropriated land" within their corporation limits.[75] In addition, Albany owned "five hundred acres of low or meadow land lying at a certain place . . . known by the name of Schaahtecogue" plus one thousand such acres at Tionnondorage.[76] The Albany corporation generally rented these extensive tracts to tenant farmers, and New York City chose to sell a large portion of its property in the late 1680s.[77]

Only occasionally did America's boroughs attempt to supplement the revenue derived from commerce and land with a poll or property tax. None of the municipal charters granted the authority to impose such a levy, but some cities obtained legislative permission to exercise this privilege for funding specific projects. Thus in 1730 provincial assemblymen authorized a municipal tax in New York City to purchase fire engines and to repair the jail, and in 1741 these legislators sanctioned a levy to fund the corporation's night watch.[78] Likewise, in 1744 Virginia's lawmakers allowed Williamsburg to impose a poll tax to finance a city prison.[79] Generally, however, America's boroughs, like those in Britain, derived their pounds and shillings not from direct taxation but from rents and licenses, and this source constituted approximately 90 percent of the municipal revenues in New York City during the 1690s.[80]

The similarity between Old World and New is also evident in the political structure of the municipal corporation. In accordance with the closed corporation model so common in England, the aldermen and councillors of Philadelphia, Williamsburg, and Norfolk served for life and replenished their own number through co-option, and the life-tenure councillors of Annapolis were chosen by popular election, unlike that city's self-elected board of aldermen.[81] The structure of New Jersey's four boroughs, New York's two cities, and Bristol, Pennsylvania, bore a closer resemblance to that of London or Norwich, with a broad electorate annually choosing the municipal aldermen and councillors.[82] The boroughs of Chester, Lancaster, and Wilmington, on the other hand, followed Berwick's example and adopted a town-meeting form of government with direct participation by the urban citizenry.[83]

Freeman status and commercial participation continued as significant factors in defining who constituted this citizenry. Thus in New York, Elizabeth, New Brunswick, and Perth Amboy, those enjoying the commercial privileges of freeman also possessed the right to vote in city elections.[84] In Philadelphia freeman status was among the eligibility requirements for municipal officeholding, and the charters of Williamsburg, Norfolk, and Annapolis required the original members of the common council to possess freeman rank.[85] Moreover, these same three corporations extended the suffrage in provincial assembly elections to those proved commercial participants who "shall hereafter have served five years to any trade within the said Borough."[86] Perhaps no measure better embodies the spirit of the commercial community than Albany's requirement that a man residing in one ward and working in another should vote and stand for office from the ward where he practiced his trade or occupation and not where he lived.[87] Commerce, not residence, defined membership in the commercial community, and thus a man acted his political role not where he ate or slept but where he produced and traded.

Despite the continuing significance of the freeman's rank, America's early boroughs did deviate from the political structure of the European commercial community. By the eighteenth century each of America's corporations granted the right of political participation not only to freemen but also to those representatives of landed interest, the freeholders. For example, under New York's charter of 1731 persons admitted to the commerce of the city no longer enjoyed the sole right to participate in municipal government but shared this privilege with owners of freeholds.[88] The charters of New Jersey's municipalities also recognized landowners as having a stake in urban government, and in Bristol, Chester, and Lancaster both freeholders and "housekeepers" enjoyed the borough franchise.[89] Likewise, in Philadelphia, Annapolis, Williamsburg, and Norfolk municipal office was open to those owning a specified value of real property as well as to freemen.[90]

Thus by the early 1700s the political monopoly of commercial participants had virtually disappeared. No longer was the electorate limited to those whom the corporation had admitted in recognition of their commercial stake in the community. Instead, the rural criterion of land as well as the urban standard of commerce had become a qualification for membership in the municipal corporation. This was only the first crack in the structure of the commercial community, but it foreshadowed the total collapse that would come in the late eighteenth and early nineteenth centuries.

Yet the question of who voted and who did not was not of such significance in 1700 as it would be in a later period, for in most municipal elections of the colonial era there was nothing resembling a party rivalry, and candidates generally faced no opposition. If an incumbent had aroused bitter animosities, an opponent might offer the electorate a choice. But such a contest was an exception. Thus municipal elections were not forums for expressing competing political ideologies, nor did the townspeople view them as a means for ensuring representative government responsible to the governed. Elections were simply one of the traditional modes for selecting officials entrusted with the prosperity and good order of the commercial community. If the men chosen proved themselves trustworthy, colonial Americans conceived of no reason to oppose them.

Representative of this phenomenon were the New Jersey borough elections of the colonial era. In 1749 the voters of New Brunswick gathered at eleven o'clock in the morning and were asked "whether anybody had anything against" the incumbent aldermen "being chosen, or whether any other Candidates were to be put up in Opposition to those." The assembled freemen expressed their support for the incumbents by acclamation, and "thus ended the Election with respect to Aldermen, without the least Contradiction or seeming Dissatisfaction shown by any Person." New Brunswick's citizens then selected the common councilmen "with Unanimity and Dispatch," and within two hours the townspeople dispersed, having unanimously chosen all the borough officers for the following year.[91] One freeman complained that the borough officials had conducted the election so rapidly that by the time he arrived the meeting was over.[92] A similar situation prevailed in the borough of Elizabeth. When Alderman Thomas Clark of Elizabeth died, a newspaper account reported that he had "been unanimously elected a magistrate of this Corporation ever since we had a charter."[93] Elizabeth had received its charter twenty-five years earlier, and thus the borough's voters appear to have unanimously elected Alderman Clark twenty-five consecutive times. If men like Clark and the New Brunswick leaders were maintaining order in the markets, punishing felons, and avoiding political feuds, they were performing their tasks competently and the townspeople saw no need to question or challenge their authority.

Even in periods of bitter political conflict, partisan competition did not long survive, and many municipal officers continued to avoid opposition. This was true in New York City during the mid-1730s, when the ambitious Lewis Morris formed a faction to rival that of Governor William Cosby. These factions battled for twelve of New York City's fourteen municipal council seats in 1734, and only the alderman and assistant alderman from the Out Ward were unopposed.[94] In the election of 1735, however, no challenger contested any of the seven incumbent aldermen, nor did anyone choose to oppose the assistant alderman in the East Ward. Morris's activities had aroused an unusual degree of political interest, and yet in 1735 only six of the fourteen council seats were contested.[95] This lack of opposition was even more pronounced in the election of 1736. According to newspaper accounts, each incumbent won reelection that year "without so much as one dissenting voice against any of them except in the Dock Ward."[96] Thus, even in a time of political tumult factional rivalry on the municipal level was short-lived, and never again during the colonial era would New Yorkers witness such a hotly contested city election as that of 1734.

Farther south in Annapolis, Maryland, contested municipal elections were also rare, and when contests did occur the authorities were irritated and confused about how to handle the situation. In 1743 a local troublemaker convinced the eminent physician Dr. Alexander Hamilton to run for city council against a man who had the backing of Maryland's governor and was described by his enemies as "a certain creature of the court." Election day found Annapolis fraught with tension and disorder. In the morning "the majority of the aldermen left the Bench in passion," and "in the afternoon the tumult was so high that the partisans went to Cudgelling and breaking of heads." Because of the violence, "the polls were shut long before they were finished or determined." Then the results were "sealed with the double seals of the Mayor and Recorder, and they have been afraid ever since to proceed upon the Election." The electoral process had failed in this colonial city as political rivalry disrupted the order and harmony which the municipal corporation sought to preserve.[97]

In Annapolis as in New York City, New Brunswick, and Elizabeth, the townspeople viewed party rivalry or political opposition not as necessary to the well-being of government but as a nuisance, a perversion, and an exceptional means which might be used in unusual situations. Municipal authorities of the seventeenth and early eighteenth centuries frowned on bitter competition at the polls just as they discouraged cutthroat competition in the marketplace. For in politics as well as economics the chief aims of the commercial community were concord, consensus, and cooperation. Municipal officials sought not to ignite the fires of controversy but to guard against any combustion of elements which might destroy order. And in their minds both the unfettered competition of political ambitions and the unrestricted competition of trade seemed highly flammable and ever destructive of the desired goal of good government.

Elections, however, were not the only means for selecting the municipal officials of colonial America. In the municipalities of Albany, New York City, New Brunswick, Perth Amboy, Burlington, and Elizabeth neither the freemen nor the aldermen elected the mayor, town clerk, sheriff, or the corporation's legal counsel, the recorder. Instead, these officials were royal appointees who owed their position to the good graces of the colonial governors.[98] This, then, was a notable deviation from the English tradition of municipal independence from the central authorities. In New York and New Jersey, unlike Great Britain, Pennsylvania, Maryland, Delaware, or Virginia, the municipal corporation was not autonomous. Rather, the provincial governors exercised vital authority over the selection of significant city officials.

This unusual arrangement originated under Dutch rule when New Netherlands' autocratic governor Peter Stuyvesant enjoyed the right to appoint the municipal officials of New Amsterdam. The English governors continued to exercise such powers after the conquest of 1664, and when Albany and New York City received charters in 1686 the political environment was not conducive to the idea of municipal autonomy. For during the 1680s Charles II and James II were seeking to expand their powers by ensuring an active royal role in borough politics. Numerous British charters of this decade reserved to the Stuart crown the right to remove municipal officers at will, and the charter of England's Chester bestowed on the monarch the authority to nominate that borough's clerk and recorder.[99] In order to mollify Whig opposition and save his toppling throne, in 1688 James II relinquished this extraordinary power over English corporations, and William and Mary later adhered to this decision. But James's proclamation did not apply to the colony of New York, and thus the crown retained its appointive power in the New World. Moreover, during the early eighteenth century New Jersey's boroughs copied the structure governing nearby Manhattan, including the provincial selection of corporation officials. Consequently, only in New Jersey and New York and not in Britain or the other colonies did the crown continue to play a role in the choice of certain borough officials, thereby perpetuating a relic of Stuart rule.

Although this royal interference compromised the traditional autonomy of the municipal corporation, still there were some limits on the power of outside officials to intervene in municipal affairs. Neither the colonial governors nor the provincial assemblies ever succeeded in amending or revoking corporate charters without the permission and encouragement of borough leaders. Provincial assemblies could grant such additional powers as the levying of a direct tax, but they would not unilaterally deprive the municipality of a charter grant of authority. For as in England, lawmakers viewed charters as inviolate and sacred compacts, not subject to the tampering of royal or legislative usurpers.[100]

Moreover, many colonial municipalities enjoyed immunity from the interference of bothersome country magistrates. As independent counties the cities of New York and Albany owed no allegiance to the officials of adjacent rural areas.[101] Likewise, Perth Amboy and New Brunswick each acquired the right to a borough sheriff, and consequently neither city was subject to the authority of law officers from surrounding Middlesex County.[102] The aldermen and councillors of Annapolis also appointed a city sheriff, thereby eliminating the need for outside interference from Maryland's officialdom.[103] In each of these cities, as in Nottingham, Norwich, and London, urban tradesmen and artisans were relatively independent of the yeomen and landlords of nearby farms and villages. For in both Old World and New, charter grantors sought to guarantee a municipal freedom conducive to the growth of commerce amid a world of agriculture.

3   The
         Yankee
         Anomaly

Tradition commanded vast loyalty in the British world of the Stuarts and early Hanoverians, but a few imaginative souls were beginning to challenge an array of sacrosanct ideas. By 1700 Harvey had nudged Galen from his pedestal, Newtonians were reshaping God in the image of their mechanistic universe, and even the municipal corporation had suffered a glancing blow. For in that deviant segment of the British world known as New England, men examined this inherited institution of urban rule and explicitly rejected it as a mode of government. Discarding the assumptions of their cousins to the south and their forefathers abroad, they felt no need for a body designed to serve the commercial demands of an urban community. Rather, they developed one institution to govern city and country alike, an institution which largely ignored the time-honored concerns of trade and industry. By doing so they severed themselves from the body of European tradition and initiated a fresh experiment in urban rule.

The basic unit of both urban and rural government in New England was the town. Unlike the municipal corporation, the New England town originated as a religious community in which only church members enjoyed the right of political participation.[1] By the late seventeenth century, however, property requirements had supplanted those of religion, with Massachusetts restricting the suffrage in town elections to persons worth twenty pounds or more.[2] Nowhere among the four New England provinces did the rank of master craftsman or the mere fact of commercial participation entitle one to a voice in the community's government. Rather, in a trading center like Boston as well as in the country villages of Dedham and Stowe, political status depended not on craft or occupation but on land and goods.

This deviation from the municipal mold is also apparent in the legislation of New England's towns. An analysis of Boston's compiled by-laws for 1701 (see table 2) reveals that only 9 percent centered on questions of fair dealing, vocational allocation, and commercial development, with the bulk of ordinances focusing on preserving safety and order and eliminating annoyances. Neither New York, Albany, nor Philadelphia could match Boston's code regulating defective chimneys, blazes on board ship, or ladders and swabs "for the quenching of fire." Likewise, Boston's ordinances against littering the streets with "shavings, filth, Soil, or Rubbish" as well as its law relating to mischievous dogs and wandering swine were comparable to the most detailed municipal measures. Yet at the same time the town of Boston maintained no public market, placed no restrictions on vocational opportunity, and enforced no standards of merchandise quality. The selectmen and town meeting did endeavor to regulate weights and measures and forbade such practices as forestalling, but the absence of easily supervised markets made the laws difficult to enforce.[3]

TABLE 2	Content Distribution of Boston's By-Laws for 1701			
	Trade	9.0%	Public Works	9.0%
	Annoyance	28.3%	Administration	13.3%
	Safety and Order	28.3%	Other	12.0%

In the field of finance a town like Boston again differed markedly from the municipalities of New York or Liverpool, since the New England town did not rely on rents or commercial tolls but acquired funds through a direct property levy known as the "town tax."[4] Since Boston maintained no public marts or commercial fairs, it could not profit from leasing stalls, renting booths, or collecting market duties. Consequently, it turned to property, not trade, for the cash necessary to sustain local government.

This gap between town and municipal corporation also extended to external relations. Boston, unlike Philadelphia, Norwich, or London, enjoyed little independence from either the surrounding county or the central authority of province and crown. For example, all town by-laws required not only town-meeting approval but also assent from the county court of quarter sessions. Since selectmen exercised no judicial authority, these same rural-oriented justices bore responsibility for enforcing town ordinances and settling commercial disputes.[5] On the provincial level, the Massachusetts General Court had the power to alter town government at will and frequently rearranged town boundaries despite vigorous opposition from a majority of the local leaders and citizens.[6] Unlike the municipal corporation, the New England town possessed no charter, and consequently notions of charter sanctity offered no protection against such meddlesome legislation.

In every aspect, then, the town polity governing Salem or Boston differed strikingly from the municipal structure which directed urban fortunes elsewhere in the British world. The town of Boston was not a commercial community governed by commercial participants for the service of trade and industry. Rather, it was a government in which commerce enjoyed no preeminent status and received little attention or sustenance. No jurisdictional wall barred rural magistrates from interfering with the alien concerns of traders and artisans, and no charter stood between the authority of local and central government. The town was instead a pliable instrument of county and province, without the power or inclination to assume the urban responsibilities shouldered by the municipal corporation.

Moreover, this application of town government to an urban center like Boston was not the result of accident or indifference. Rather, it was a consequence of careful debate and consideration in both the provincial assembly and the town meeting. By the mid-eighteenth century, each of these bodies had reviewed the respective merits of the town and the municipal corporation and had specifically rejected the latter as an instrument of urban rule. For New Englanders had grown accustomed to the freedom of unfettered commerce and the privilege of direct participation in town meetings, and they were not ready to sacrifice these for a government of aldermen, councillors, markets, and monopolies. Unlike the men of New York and Philadelphia, suspicious Bostonians saw no benevolence in a government which determined economic opportunity and restricted the right to sell and manufacture. Instead, they perceived in the municipal corporation the possibility of power misused and the danger of despotic regulation.

The first body to question traditional municipal government was the Massachusetts General Court. In 1650 Boston's town meeting petitioned this provincial legislature for approval of a submitted corporate charter, and the general court agreed to "grant the petitioners a corporation if the articles or terms . . . thereof were so presented as rationally should appear respecting the mean condition of the Country."[7] The court thus postponed action on the subject and also refused to take any definitive action on the petitions for incorporation which Bostonians submitted in 1659, 1661, 1662, 1663, and 1677.[8] During these early years of settlement the people of Boston seemed to favor adopting a corporate charter, but the provincial authorities procrastinated, hesitated, and delayed.

The charter which Bostonians submitted to the court described a typical Old World corporation complete with those economic restrictions and regulations so central to the municipal government. Under the proposed charter, the "voices only of the freeman" would annually elect a mayor, six aldermen, and twelve councillors. Once chosen these officials would possess the authority to enact ordinances for "the better carrying on of Trade and Traffic . . . and the true making of all sorts of Wares" as well as by-laws ensuring that "one Trade, Mystery or Occupation not intrude or entrench upon another." Moreover, the mayor and aldermen would "assess all abuses, disorders and oppressions in the assize of bread and measure of Ale and Beer, and all other weights and measures whatsoever" and seek to ensure that all goods "may be obtained at reasonable rates."[9] During the mid-seventeenth century, then, Bostonians were attempting to create a municipal corporation very similar to those they had known in Norfolk, Essex, or Kent.

But this aping of Old World forms was not to win the approval of provincial lawmakers. Massachusetts leaders wished to preserve the town-meeting form of government, together with the free movement of labor and goods throughout the colony. Artisans from surrounding towns may have especially feared efforts to exclude outside competition, and rural shoemakers had already petitioned the general court in protest against "our Brethen in Boston" having power "put into their hands to hinder a free trade" and bar "Country Shoemakers from Coming into the Market."[10] Thus despite the urgings of Boston's inhabitants, New England's largest urban center continued to operate as a town and not as a municipal corporation.

During the first decade of the eighteenth century, the issue again arose, but this time the controversy over incorporation centered not in the provincial assembly but in the Boston town meeting. In December 1708, Boston's selectmen proposed the adoption of municipal government as a solution to the problem of outside interference, complaining specifically that the town's by-laws were unenforceable so long as the "Execution of Town orders" rested in "the hands of Justices only, who are not Town but County officers."[11] A committee assumed the task of drafting a charter, and three months later they submitted this document to a hostile town meeting. One critic present at the gathering denounced incorporation, crying, "It is a whelp now—it will be a Lion By and by. Knock it in the head." The majority of Bostonians agreed with these sentiments and proceeded to deliver such a knock in the form of an overwhelming negative vote.[12]

Defeat, however, did not silence the critics of town government, and debate on the subject continued throughout the next decade. During these years, advocates of change lauded incorporation as a means for bringing justice, organization, and prosperity into urban life. Their foes consistently emphasized the threat municipal government posed to the political rights and economic liberties of each Bostonian. Thus one argument centered on the prospect of order and equity, whereas the other focused on the likelihood of overbearing authority and excessive control.

Prominent among the advocates of order and regulation was the Reverend Benjamin Colman. During the early decades of the eighteenth century, Colman spearheaded a fight to establish public markets and thereby eliminate the inconvenience resulting from the absence of fixed commercial facilities. Under existing conditions, each vendor wasted time and effort trotting "about the Town crying at every Corner what he has to sell" while "our very Gentry" traipsed "to the Ends of Town to get a little butter or a few Eggs for their Families." According to Colman, housewives never knew where to find provisions, and vendors were equally uncertain about the location of prospective customers. Consequently buyers wandered the streets in search of sellers while sellers walked the pavements in pursuit of buyers.[13]

Colman also claimed that such peripatetic trading seriously undermined efforts to eliminate fraud and unsavory price fixing. Without markets and municipal supervisors, Bostonians suffered from the knavery of "Hucksters forestalling, engrossing and buying up the Provisions that come into Town." Thus the poor were forced to "parcel out a cruel pittance" to those crafty dealers who "buy almost at any rate and then raise the price again as they please." Borough leaders in Britain, New York, Pennsylvania, and Virginia had attempted to prevent such inequities by establishing strictly supervised markets, but as yet Bostonians had failed to act.[14]

Underlying this resistance to change was a widespread fear of governmental interference, and the possibility of craft restrictions and commercial codes did not arouse universal favor or enthusiasm. For almost eighty years Bostonians had profited from their peculiar form of commercial anarchy, and now they confronted a future of order and regulation with fear and misgiving.

The idea of restricted vocational opportunity especially offended Boston's citizens, eliciting angry protests from the town's obstreperous pamphleteers. According to one critic, incorporation would allow the mayor and aldermen "to Let in or Keep out" whichever traders they pleased, and not even "An honest Man may . . . come into the Town without buying his Freedom."[15] This same spokesman further claimed that municipal rule would result in artisans' "being reduced to manage but one Trade," a reform "Unsupportable in its difficulties." For in unregulated Boston "Shopkeepers . . . do many of them occupy more than Twelve Trades and the Handicraftsmen as many as their Genius and Stock do lead them to." According to this critic, some storekeepers sold more hats than did the hatters themselves. Yet once Boston obtained a charter of incorporation, "from that day no Shopkeeper might Sell a Hat."[16]

Another pamphleteer expressed similar sentiments in favor of unrestricted vocational opportunity. He lauded the existing town government for permitting craftsmen to pursue "one or more Callings as they shall find most conducing to their own Welfare." Moreover, he cited the economic growth of Boston as proof of the wisdom of past policy. "What an instance . . . of Folly and Levity in a People," he proclaimed, "for them to Change a government under which they have thus prospered." If this change of government did actually occur, the result would be "utter Ruin, Confusion & Undoing."[17] Repeatedly Bostonians spoke of a dire future in which city officials would determine who traded and who did not and who practiced as butcher and who as tanner. This world of regulation was not one they envied, and through debate in town meeting and pamphlet rhetoric they sought to bar its realization.

Similarly, the notion of public markets did not appeal to most Bostonians. Many consumers feared that market trading would result in higher prices, and vendors believed it would seriously reduce profits.[18] One pamphleteer predicted that traders would refuse to bring their provisions to a public mart but would instead sell their goods in the unregulated towns of Roxbury and Charlestown. And another believed that incorporation would drive "out the Trade of this Town to its neighbouring Towns, & so make them Rich & Happy and this Poor and Miserable."[19] On a more abstract plane, still others protested market regulations as "a breach upon their natural rights and liberties." These men would "go where we will and sell how we will" without concern for equity in the distribution of goods or opportunities.[20] For such traders freedom was of preeminent concern, barring any sympathy for the excessive government of the municipal corporation.

The townspeople's views on political structure also reflected this fear of broad public authority. Throughout the colonial era the men of Boston remained dedicated to the ideal of simple, direct government—government in which each man's political contribution would be great while his financial obligation was small. They desired a structure that would obviate the necessity for costly pageantry and administration while preserving the traditional right of an individual to vent his grievances in common assembly. With these aims in mind, Boston's citizens judged the alternative forms of urban government and rendered a verdict in favor of the town.

In an effort to influence this decision, local pamphleteers carefully contrasted the thrift and simplicity of a New England town with the financial burden of a complex municipal corporation. According to one writer, incorporation would entail maintaining "a keeper of Two Great Silver Maces, . . . a Sword Bearer, a Clerk of the Court, a Clerk of the Market, a Recorder, [and] a Chamberlain," while frugal town government would continue to operate without the expense of any such costly officialdom.[21] Another pamphleteer likewise praised the town as "a Government the least . . . expensive of . . . any Government whatsoever," while damning the municipal corporation for the "loss of Time & Money" resulting from its "Needless, Childish, and troublesome Formalities." In this man's opinion, the town had all the advantages of a corporation "without being at any of the Charges Corporations are at To Support their Magistrates."[22] On every page the image presented was the same. The town appeared as an exemplar of fiscal care and the municipal corporation as a model of frivolity and waste.

In like manner, these same writers fought to preserve direct participation in the town meeting and thwart the introduction of government by elected representatives. Thus one pamphleteer lauded the existing town-meeting structure as "the greatest and most precious Privilege any Town or Society can be possessed of" while direly predicting that "the Rich will exert the Right of Dominion" in a government of aldermen and councillors. With the advent of the municipal corporation, Boston would bid "Farewell to all Town Meetings and to the Management of the Town Affairs by the Freeholders Collectively." According to this writer, "the Great Men will no more have the Dissatisfaction of seeing their Poorer Neighbours stand up for equal Privileges with them in the highest Acts of Town Government." Instead, under corporate rule these "Great Men" will gain control, and "Rich & Poor Men then will no more be jumbled together in Town Offices."[23]

Another writer claimed that incorporation would result in the delegation of governmental authority to "Rich Covetous Mayors" and an abandonment of "the Ancient Rights and undoubted Property of our Voting at Town Meetings." In this man's opinion, the people of Boston should not delegate authority but instead should adhere to the maxim, "If you would have your work well done, do it yourself." Consequently he urged Bostonians to reject the municipal plan projected by men who "like . . . the Great Fish" wish to serve as "lords over the Small, to make them to observe their Motions, and also in part to live upon them."[24] Men like this writer wished to maintain an open political forum just as they desired to ensure an unrestricted marketplace. And in their opinion, neither was possible under the government of a municipal corporation.

Such attitudes prevailed throughout the colonial period, defeating all subsequent proposals for the reform of Boston's government. In 1734, however, the town meeting did compromise on the subject of market control, approving the establishment of three marts and an accompanying code of regulation.[25] Yet this change of heart was short-lived, and soon the townspeople succeeded in emasculating the regulative scheme. As early as 1736 the town meeting voted to dismiss all market clerks and thereby eliminate the supervisory personnel necessary for collecting market fees and enforcing quality and quantity standards.[26] Moreover, Bostonians generally refused to shop at the markets, and the newly constructed stalls stood empty and unused. Door-to-door peddling had become a way of life in Boston, and the citizens did not adapt readily to the idea of a public mart.

In March 1737 a violent mob completed the task of destroying Boston's public market system. The mob marched on the town's three market houses, leveling one and sawing through the foundations of another.[27] One month later Boston's town meeting responded to this violence with a resolution permanently closing the damaged facilities and ordering that these buildings "shall Be Appropriated to some other Use."[28] Boston had thus attempted to conform to the commercial pattern which prevailed throughout the remainder of Christendom, but the attempt had failed.

Five years later the town did deign to accept the gift of a market house from Peter Faneuil by a close vote of 367 to 360. But the community accepted Faneuil's generous offer only with the understanding that strolling vendors might continue to "be at liberty to carry their Marketing wheresoever they please about the town."[29] Bostonians were unswerving in their prejudice against markets during the following three decades, and the empty stalls of Faneuil Hall stood as a visible reminder of the persistent antagonism toward the commercial strictures and trading codes of the Old World municipality. The rhetoric extolling economic liberty persisted, and New Englanders continued to insist that market regulations should "not deprive us of the liberty common to Englishmen."[30]

Such behavior and attitudes may have been an anomaly in the early eighteenth century, but they were soon to become the norm. For by the 1730s and 1740s a new era of urban rule was dawning, an era that would supersede the age of the commercial community. During this era the concerns which had motivated Bostonians as early as 1700 would become preeminent in the minds of men throughout the English-speaking world. Thus Boston's views on incorporation did not simply represent a curious dead end in the history of municipal government. Instead, Boston was to be the birthplace of a new attitude toward urban rule, an attitude emphasizing greater economic freedom and broader participation in local government. The libertarian views expressed by Bostonians would gain wide credence by the end of the century, and among the consequences would be a marked change in the municipal structure. New England, in other words, had developed an alternative to the inherited approach of the municipal corporation. It was this alternative outlook that gradually enveloped the rest of the English-speaking world and spelled an end to the traditional structure of urban rule. Yankee resistance to corporate government was not simply a meaningless anomaly but a precursor of fresh, bold change, a precursor of that spirit which remolded the municipal corporation and fashioned it into the urban polity of today.

2   The
     Municipal
     Revolution

4   Toward a New Pattern

In 1727 Philadelphia's common council permanently tabled a proposal for better enforcing the freeman's privilege and abandoned forever the policy of exclusionary trading rights.[1] Two decades later London's councillors also turned away from tradition and unanimously voted to permit each master craftsman "to employ any Number of Non-Freemen to work under him."[2] A century earlier such actions would have been unthinkable, but by the 1730s and 1740s a revolution was festering that would eventually destroy the traditional municipality and erect in its place a new edifice of urban government. This fresh structure would be one in which concerns of health, safety, streets, and lighting outweighed those of monopolies, markets, price-fixing, and commercial chicanery. Moreover, political power would rest not in the hands of corporation-admitted traders and artisans but would belong to all adult males residing within the corporation limits. This would be not a commercial community but a residential one, governed by residents for the safety and convenience of all the city's inhabitants and not simply for the service of commercial participants. Not until the 1830s would this new form reach maturity in both Britain and America; but as early as the mid-eighteenth century the change had begun.

Underlying this transformation was a radical shift in the economic and demographic facts of urban life. The advent of industrialism pushed Britain's urban population to unprecedented heights, and the lure of America induced a similar growth in England's colonial cities. Liverpool's population rose fivefold during the first half of the eighteenth century, that of Philadelphia and New York City increased approximately threefold, and the number of Sheffield's inhabitants soared from 2,695 in 1736 to 12,571 in 1755.[3] As thousands of migrants flooded the towns and boroughs of the British world, the difficulties of enforcing exclusionary privileges increased markedly. No longer were Britain's

boroughs tight, regulated communities dedicated to the neat allocation of economic opportunity. Instead they were labor-hungry
hubs of industry and trade in dire need of all workers, freeman or
nonfreeman.[4] These cities were growing rapidly in wealth and
population, and the force of this expansion would soon level the
ancient barriers of municipal regulation.

A second threat to urban tradition came from the less tangible
realm of ideas. Whiggish notions of personal liberty which had
been so prevalent in Boston were now causing men throughout
Britain and America to question the justice of municipal restrictions
on individual ambition. As early as 1749 the Scottish thinker Adam
Smith was arguing that "little else is required to carry a state to the
highest degree of affluence . . . but peace, easy taxes and a toler-
able administration of justice: all the rest being brought about by
the natural course of things."[5] In the 1770s Smith applied this belief
in the natural order, together with his libertarian ideals, to a
systematic study of economics and established himself as chief
prophet of a new faith in entrepreneurial freedom. According to
Smith's landmark study *Wealth of Nations*, "the pretence that
corporations are necessary for the better government of . . . trade
is without any foundation'; and the popularity of this laissez-faire
gospel soon spelled doom for past policies of municipal supervision.[6]

Bolstering this ideological impetus for change was a new feeling
of optimism, contrasting markedly with the pessimistic mentality
underlying traditional trade regulation. Whereas past generations
had viewed scarcity as an economic constant and pestilence as
inevitable, people in the eighteenth century were gradually recog-
nizing the possibility of material growth and worldly advancement.
By the 1770s the introduction of improved livestock breeds,
methods of crop rotation, and new varieties of fodder had markedly increased the food supply of Britain and put an end to fears of
famine. Expanding food production in the colonies also limited the
threat of starvation, and never again would Albany and New York
City suffer a bread famine like that of 1696. Likewise, the efforts of
Lady Mary Montague and Cotton Mather to overcome the dangers
of smallpox through inoculation had demonstrated man's ability
to master the threatening forces of nature. Englishmen in both
Britain and America were finally making substantial gains in the war
for human survival, and the success of their efforts encouraged

others to engage in schemes aimed at bettering man's worldly existence. "A general spirit prevails for correcting ancient errors and establishing new improvements," one Englishman observed in 1771, and together with the belief in personal liberty this spirit would lead men to discard the traditional pattern of urban rule.[7]

Thus the mental and material framework of Western life was changing, and the evolution of municipal institutions reflected this change. By 1775 economic scarcity no longer dominated urban thinking, whereas the prospect of economic growth did. Consequently corporate barriers to growth, mobility, and enterprise gradually collapsed. Meanwhile man's confidence in medical science was growing steadily, producing an increased emphasis on municipal health programs. And as the urban standard of living rose during the early days of the industrial revolution, people demanded better streets, improved public lighting, and more adequate fire protection. Slowly the municipal corporation was adjusting to an emerging atmosphere of confidence, expansion, and liberty—an atmosphere alien to the commercial restrictions of the past and conducive to change in the future.

Among the first restrictions to disappear were those allocating vocational opportunity. Albany enacted its last ordinance concerning the freeman's commercial monopoly in 1724, and in 1755 reformers in New Brunswick were contending that "no one of any Trade was obliged to take up his Freedom."[8] By mid-century New York City's corporation had also abandoned efforts to ensure traditional exclusionary practices. Thus, of fifty-four artisans advertising in the *New-York Mercury* during the year 1753, only thirty could claim the time-honored status of freeman.[9] Across the Atlantic the councillors of Dover in 1747 took the unprecedented step of hiring as a municipal construction crew "such bricklayers as will work cheapest, whether they be Freemen or not."[10] Southampton's magistrates likewise ceased to enforce exclusionary trading privileges after 1750, and in 1758 the aldermen of Leicester prosecuted their last commercial interloper.[11] Occasionally city fathers in both England and America attempted to revive exclusionary measures, and as late as 1787 Albany's magistrates agreed to "meet every Monday and Wednesday . . . for the express purpose of carrying into Execution that clause in the Charter . . . which prohibits all Persons but Freemen to Trade in the City."[12] Such efforts, however, were short-lived and without notable effect.

By 1775 the trading monopoly that had been so common in both England and America no longer played a significant role in the municipal government of Britain's empire. Albany's control of the fur trade was also a casualty of this new era. Since 1686 the city's councillors and aldermen had endeavored to enforce the charter provision which required Indian traders to conduct their bartering solely within the Albany corporation limits. Traders from nearby Schenectady had long opposed this restriction on their vocational freedom, and finally in 1723 Johannes Myndertse challenged Albany's monopoly in the provincial courts. The municipal sheriff had arrested Myndertse for trading with Indians in his Schenectady home rather than in the Albany stockade. Myndertse, however, retaliated by commencing action in the provincial Supreme Court and charged the city's aldermen with trespass and false imprisonment.[13] The aldermen persisted in defending Albany's monopoly and passed a resolution "that no licenses be granted to the Indian Traders at Schenectady . . . nor to any . . . others to the north of this city."[14] After four years of litigation, however, the Supreme Court in 1727 ruled in favor of the Schenectady dissidents, striking down the restraints imposed by Albany's corporation.[15] From that date forward dealers could barter their furs and trinkets anywhere they pleased, and most chose sites far from the surveillance of urban magistrates.

Meanwhile, in New York City and Philadelphia municipal leaders were also abandoning efforts to ensure vocational standards and the quality of manufacturing workmanship. In 1711 New York City's councillors had required boys to serve a full seven years as apprentices in order to improve the quality of local crafts, and the city's master artisans had complied with this ruling. Twenty years later, however, the common council dropped the seven-year provision, and never again would it impose standards on apprenticeship education.[16] Philadelphia's municipal leaders also found it necessary to accept shoddy workmanship during this period. Their efforts to establish guild companies for the improvement of craft standards had generally proved unsuccessful, and only the city's carpenters had formed a lasting trade organization.[17] Municipal magistrates continued to register apprenticeship indentures and protect consumers against fraudulent merchandise, but they no longer enacted ambitious measures aimed at upgrading the quality of handicraft goods.

Although municipalities such as Albany, Philadelphia, and New York abandoned their regulation of vocational opportunity and manufacturing standards, they continued to exercise considerable authority over pricing and public markets. For example, in 1754 the borough of Norfolk authorized the drafting of an ordinance regulating the cost not only of bread, but also of "Beef, Veal, Mutton, Lamb, Shoat, Goose, Turkeys, Fowls, Duck Eggs, Butter ... and Meal."[18] Albany enacted a similarly comprehensive scheme for price-fixing in 1756, and in 1763 New York City granted municipal officials the power to determine the cost of all meat, fish, and dairy products sold in the public market.[19] Moreover, the corders, gaugers, and packers of America's municipalities persisted throughout the period in their efforts to eliminate commercial shysters and cheats from the urban market place. Thus municipal leaders were only gradually veering from the path of tradition as they continued to protect the buyer and ceased to hamstring the producer.

Some urban retailers, however, were growing increasingly dissatisfied with the broad price-fixing and market powers of the municipality. For example, in 1763 New York City's butchers reacted sharply to the newly imposed restrictions on meat prices. Refusing to accept the city council's rate schedule, the majority of butchers combined with disgruntled stock raisers from the surrounding counties and agreed to suspend all meat sales until the restrictive ordinance was repealed. One rebellious member of the trade proclaimed that he would sell his beef at whatever price he wished "in spite of all the *wise heads* that made the law could do."[20] Others expressed a similar contempt for the corporation, and there arose a heated debate over the merits and demerits of municipal price regulations and market controls.

Advocates of the price-fixing measure complained of "the impositions of the butchers and the extravagent demands of some of our country people." "Why," they asked, "should this city be under the peculiar curse of being fleeced ... by the butcher?"[21] And they believed that the exercise of legal force was necessary to correct this situation and protect the public from the power of the greedy tradesmen. According to men of this opinion, "compulsion must be called in to remedy the defect" and restore a balance of economic power.[22]

The butchers and market vendors resorted to more libertarian rhetoric in pleading their case. Applying the Whiggish notions of liberty to the economic as well as the political sphere, they proclaimed themselves "friends to the liberty of *Englishmen*." They argued that "we were born free Englishmen and had the liberty, as such, to sell our own effects at our own liberty."[23] Unlike the bakers and carters of an earlier period, they were not simply seeking an upward adjustment of rates but were challenging the very authority of the municipality to regulate prices. In the end the butchers abandoned this extreme position and agreed to accept a revised price schedule, but their defiance showed an emerging discontent.

This gradual shift in attitude is also evident from an analysis of ordinances for the late colonial period. In Lancaster, Albany, and New York City trade regulation continued to be the primary concern of municipal legislators, but it no longer demanded such a disproportionate share of their attention (see table 3). Whereas the figures in the trade column ranged from 53 to 60 percent for the period 1705–24, by the last decades of the colonial era these figures had dropped to a range of 39 to 48 percent. On the other hand, the percentages in the column headed "public safety and order" tripled for both New York City and Albany during this period, rising from 8 and 11 percent to 24 and 33 percent. Gradually America's councillors were stepping up their efforts against those evils which had long threatened urban health and property. Employing the resources of the municipal corporation, they now hoped to lessen the ravages of fire, disease, and crime and make the city a safer place to live.[24]

This new initiative was most evident in fire protection. As of 1700 Boston's brigade was the only fire company in the English colonies,

TABLE 3   Content Distribution of City Ordinances, 1742–73

Content	Lancaster 1742–59	Albany 1773	New York City 1773
Trade	42.7%	39.4%	47.6%
Annoyance	23.7%	6.5%	8.6%
Public Safety and Order	24.1%	33.3%	23.5%
Public Works	0	3.9%	2.5%
Administration	0.8%	8.5%	9.0%
Other	8.7%	8.4%	8.7%

and the chief tool for extinguishing blazes remained the simple water bucket. By the close of the colonial period, however, most municipalities possessed both an organized battalion of fire fighters and at least one up-to-date pumping engine.

Typical of municipal efforts were the measures taken by the common council of New York City. New York did not obtain its first fire engine until 1731, when the aldermen and councillors agreed to order "Mr. Newsham's New Invention . . . with suctions, Leathern Pipes and Caps and Other Materials."[25] In 1736 the council expressed further interest in the subject by appropriating ten pounds to a local gunsmith "to Enable him to go on with finishing A small fire Engine he is making for an Experiment."[26] By 1753 the old-fashioned engines no longer sufficed, and a local newspaper complained "we are . . . in want of at least one engine of the largest size, which throws water about one hundred and seventy feet high."[27] The common council, however, added more engines to the fleet, and in 1776 the corporation could boast of eight such pumping machines as well as two hook-and-ladder wagons. A corps of 170 volunteers operated this machinery, and the corporation hired a salaried engineer and three assistants to coordinate men and equipment.[28]

Albany's municipal leaders followed this example and sought to considerably improve the quality of municipal fire protection. In 1731 the city fathers decided "that an Engine or Water Spout be sent for to England per the first opportunity in the Spring." They obtained such a machine with a sucking pipe six feet in length and a forty-foot leather hose to extinguish the frequent blazes that endangered the community. In 1741 the city council built an engine house and hired three firemen at a salary of six schepels of wheat a year (about four bushels).[29] By the close of the colonial era, the city had both a fleet of engines and a group of capable firemen.

Other cities developed similar armies of fire fighters trained to man advanced equipment. Philadelphia's corporation purchased the city's first fire engine as early as 1718, and by 1730 the common council "agreed that three Engines be purchased . . . and sent for to England . . . and Two Hundred Buckets, Twenty ladders, and Twenty-five Hooks, with axes, be purchased here."[30] By the 1770s a hierarchy of corporation-appointed directors and subdirectors governed the four fire companies of Annapolis, Maryland; New Brunswick's corporation owned two up-to-date fire engines; and

Norfolk's municipal leaders had also purchased the latest machinery, hired men to care for it, and erected a shed to shelter the equipment.[31] For centuries fire had ravaged the shops and homes of the world's great cities, and finally the municipal corporation was effectively combating this menace.

Questions of health and sickness likewise received greater attention during the mid-eighteenth century. Before this, borough fathers had occasionally taken emergency action when confronted with the threat of epidemic, but they rarely endeavored to provide permanent nursing facilities or to engage in long-term efforts to eradicate the sources of disease.[32] In 1764, however, the Virginia legislature authorized Williamsburg's corporation to raise money for a hospital "for the reception of any person or persons who may be hereafter found within the said city infected with contagious distempers."[33] A year later Annapolis's municipal government also embarked on a program to combat contagion, enacting a by-law which penalized inhabitants who "introduce or bring the Small Pox into this City by Inoculation."[34] Similarly, both New York City and Albany licensed and regulated midwives, requiring of them an oath pledging "to help every Woman labouring of child, as well the Poor as the Rich" and not to "suffer any Woman's Child to be murdered, maimed, or otherwise hurt."[35]

Some city residents favored an even broader attack on disease and suggested certain sanitation measures as an answer to the community's health problems. For example, in 1743–44 Cadwallader Colden urged New York's corporation to lessen the threat of fever by cleaning up the city's slips and draining stagnant water from cellars and pits.[36] Responding to these comments, the municipality instituted a program to combat "the noisome Vapours and Smells" by which "Distempers of many Kinds are . . . occasioned." In order to ensure "the Purity of the Air" and prevent such disease-ridden odors, the corporation forbade anyone within a specified area of Manhattan to "have, use, make or keep any Vat or Pits of Standing Water, whether for Tanners, Skinners, Leather-Dressers, Curriers, [or] Glovers."[37] As yet the public health movement was in its nascent stage, but this ordinance reveals a growing concern among municipal leaders for the physical safety of America's people.

Colonial aldermen further sought to upgrade the quality of life by devoting a portion of municipal expenditures to lighting city thoroughfares. Of America's municipalities only New York City maintained any system of street illumination during the early eighteenth century, and even there the corporation did nothing more than require householders to hang out lanterns.[38] In 1762, however, New York's aldermen and councillors abandoned this reliance on the citizenry and initiated a program whereby the corporation rather than the individual would assume responsibility for erecting lamp-posts throughout the city.[39] Norfolk followed New York's example in 1765, and Albany's corporation soon did likewise, purchasing twenty streetlamps in 1771.[40] By the close of the colonial period, America's municipal leaders had accepted the necessity of public illumination and had progressed substantially toward the objective of safe, lighted streets.

At the same time America's boroughs were assuming these costly responsibilities, they were also acquiring fresh sources of revenue. For example, in 1763 and 1764 Virginia's legislators granted Williamsburg and Norfolk the authority to levy direct taxes for the support of such programs as lighting, fire fighting, policing, and paving.[41] In 1753, 1761, and 1774 New York's assembly passed similar authorizations for New York City and Albany, thereby ensuring revenue for purchasing streetlamps and sinking public wells.[42] Such poll or property levies accounted for an ever increasing portion of municipal funds and generously supplemented the traditional revenues derived from commercial tolls, rents, and licenses. By 1775 market exactions, wharf fees, and freeman's charges no longer occupied such a prominent place in city financing, as other forms of taxation were gradually becoming the mainstay of the municipality.

These changes in the nature of municipal taxation and legislation were as evident in Britain as they were in America. In 1744 Leicester appropriated forty pounds for the purchase of "Mr. Newsham's new invented Engines for Extinguishing fire" and employed twenty men to keep this machinery in order.[43] Eleven years later the city of Lincoln obtained its first fire engine, and in 1763 Parliament granted York's corporation the power to levy a tax for erecting street-lamps.[44] Liverpool's aldermen were especially vigorous and innovative, initiating programs for widening and cleaning streets, erecting lamps, and laying out public gardens.[45] In Britain as in America, material expectations were rising, and the urban dweller of 1775 demanded a far wider range of municipal services than had his ancestors of 1600 or 1700. Consequently, the priorities of city government were gradually shifting as concerns of safety moved to center stage and questions of trade and commerce slowly exited.

This expansion of municipal function, however, was not uniform throughout the cities and boroughs of Britain and America. Whereas many municipal corporations adjusted to this new age, others reacted to change with lethargy and indifference. In these boroughs, the municipal leaders concentrated their efforts on managing corporation properties and neglected both the traditional tasks of trade regulation and the newer duties of safety and public works. Such men did not meet the challenge of the times but rather sought to evade any further burdens or responsibilities.

Typifying men of this attitude were the councillors of Philadelphia and of Coventry. During the mid-eighteenth century Philadelphia's corporation generally ignored its governmental functions, enacting only one new ordinance between 1740 and 1776.[46] Yet the city's rulers revealed no such lethargy when confronted with a wharf lease or the possibility of acquiring an additional parcel of land. For example, in 1753 the corporation showed rare vigor in its attempt to assume ownership of the Blue Anchor Landing, and in 1758 it acted with inordinate speed when faced with the lucrative prospect of leasing the city's burial ground as pasturage.[47] Across the Atlantic, the aldermen and councillors of Coventry were equally avaricious and insensitive to public needs. The bulk of that city's municipal revenue went not for streets or even markets but for lavish corporation banquets and generous perquisites. Moreover, the leaders of the eighteenth-century Coventry were notoriously dishonest and felt few qualms about pilfering from the charitable trusts under their care.[48] These men, like their Philadelphia counterparts, did not wish to extend the limits of municipal endeavor but sought to withdraw from public service and concentrate on accumulating corporate and personal income.

As the Philadelphia corporation became increasingly lethargic, it also grew increasingly inbred and isolated from the changing currents of the time. By 1776 the city council had developed into an incestuous association dominated by members of a relatively few wealthy families. Eighty-five percent of the corporation members admitted between 1727 and 1776 were related to another member, as a bevy of sons, brothers, sons-in-law, and brothers-in-law achieved seats on the municipal council. William Allen served as a member of the corporation from 1728 to 1774, during which time his two brothers-in-law and three sons acquired council seats, and two of these sons also married daughters of corporation members.[49] Colonial Philadelphia was booming with an influx of immigrants of varied backgrounds, ideas, and interests, but the municipal corporation was not responding to this change. Instead, the only new faces on the city council bore a striking family resemblance to the old ones.

During these same years, Philadelphia's inbred oligarchs were also becoming permanently estranged from electoral politics and popular opinion. In the first quarter-century of the municipality's existence corporation officials had frequently run for such elective posts as provincial assemblyman and had curried the favor of the Pennsylvania citizenry. But by the 1750s and 1760s municipal leaders were eschewing participation in the elected provincial assembly and instead accepting seats on the provincial council, an appointed body selected by Pennsylvania's governor. From 1701 to 1726 an average of 4.5 corporation members served each year in the assembly, whereas during the years 1750 to 1775 only 2.5 annually held seats in that elected body. Yet 20 of the 26 men appointed to the provincial council after 1726 also occupied positions in Philadelphia's municipal government and helped guide the policy of the corporation.[50] Corporation members continued to exercise a significant influence in provincial government, but not as a result of popular, electoral support.

By the final years of the colonial era Philadelphia's corporation was no longer receptive to fresh blood among its membership or fresh ideas from the popular electorate. It was an exclusive body of prosperous gentlemen, and 65 percent of those attending council meetings in the early 1770s ranked within the top 5 percent of all Philadelphians in terms of wealth.[51] Such golden names as Shippen, Chew, Powell, and Willing ornamented the roster of corporation leaders, but not one of these prominent figures endeavored to revitalize the listless municipal council. While population soared and ideas on politics and the economy changed, Philadelphia's self-elected elite went through the motions of governing, indifferent to the needs or interests of the people.

To provide the essential programs neglected by these aldermen and their British counterparts, Parliament and the Pennsylvania Assembly established a series of independent statutory authorities known as "improvement" commissions. In 1751 Philadelphia's corporation ceded control over the night watch to one such commission, and eleven years later a similar organization took charge of the city's streets.[52] Parliament established this same type of board in virtually all of England's major cities to upgrade the quality of such services as paving, lighting, and crime protection. In Leeds, Chester, Oxford, and Philadelphia the commissioners were popularly elected, whereas in Coventry, Northampton, and Winchester the time-honored principle of co-option prevailed.[53] Yet no matter the mode of selection, each of these bodies represented a radical departure from the tradition of urban rule. For in the past, men had relied solely on the municipal corporation to perform the governmental functions of city life. Now lawmakers were bypassing the corporation and turning to alternative forms better adapted to the demands of a new age.

The legislators of North Carolina, Virginia, and Maryland also applied this commission mode of government to the rule of smaller, unchartered trading centers. For example, Virginia's assembly created life-tenure boards to govern the villages of Alexandria, Fredericksburg, and Winchester, and similar bodies ruled such settlements as Baltimore, Maryland, and Charlotte and Edenton, North Carolina.[54] Before 1763 Wilmington and New Bern, North Carolina, also possessed this form of government, but in these communities the freeholders enjoyed the privilege of annually electing the ruling board of commissioners.[55] Unlike the street authority of London or the night watch commission of Philadelphia, the village bodies of Virginia, Maryland, and North Carolina assumed a wide range of duties, including the construction of markets and wharfs and the surveying of thoroughfares. Yet these broad-purpose village commissions and the more limited improvement authorities did share one basic attribute. Each derived its power not from an inviolate grant of privilege but from a simple statute alterable at the will of a legislative majority. These commissions were not municipal corporations acting under a royal concession of power but flexible instruments through which a central legislature might serve the changing needs and demands of the period.

Thus new modes of urban government were developing as certain municipal corporations failed to adapt to fresh needs and desires. An economic and political revolution was beginning to sweep the Western world, a revolution that emphasized the liberation of the individual and held an optimistic vision of man's ability to harness nature. Urban residents now demanded that government take greater action against such natural threats as disease and fire, and corporations and commissions in both Britain and America were generally responding to these demands. Likewise, an increasing number of people were restive under the restraints placed on individual economic freedom, and some ancient restrictions were slowly disappearing. But in the municipal corporations of Philadelphia or Coventry, limitations on political participation remained as indifferent oligarchs continued to govern.

Even in the more energetic municipalities, authority became increasingly ingrown and isolated as long-term incumbents ruled confidently amid the popular tumult engulfing Britain's colonies. By the 1760s and 1770s cries against government authority had reached a shrill peak, and slogans such as "no taxation without representation" were on the lips of thousands of Americans. Yet the municipal councils were generally not in the vanguard of this protest movement. In fact, during the early 1770s a number of America's corporations appeared to be veering away from the much-vaunted ideal of government strictly responsible to the will of the taxpaying public.

Just as Philadelphia's oligarchs were hostile to popular participation during the late colonial period, so the corporation leaders of New York City sought to limit the public's access to local rule. In 1770 the aldermen and councillors of New York City voted "that the doors of the Common Council Chamber for the future be Shut during their Sitting" and thereby prohibited townspeople from attending the council meetings.[56] New Yorkers had previously enjoyed this privilege, and in the 1730s the council had defeated an attempt to exclude observers.[57] But by 1770 New York's municipal leaders no longer relished the scrutiny of their constituents, and the council doors were now to remain shut.

In Lancaster and Norfolk the magistrates displayed a similar desire to limit popular participation in city government. In 1772 Lancaster's borough council proposed a charter amendment that would eliminate the town-meeting type of direct participation and place legislative authority solely in the hands of the councilmen. According to Lancaster's officials, "the Consent of the Majority of the Inhabitants to any Ordinances or Rules" was "very inconvenient if not impracticable," and they favored a mode "less troublesome."[58]

In Virginia municipal leaders also showed little enthusiasm for broad public participation in government even though they ardently supported the struggle to ensure colonial liberties. Norfolk's mayor had led a mob protesting parliamentary tyranny in the form of the Stamp Act, and yet in 1774 that city's magistrates refused to accede to a petition asking for popular election of councillors rather than the closed corporation system of co-option.[59] In neither Norfolk nor Lancaster did urban rulers share the growing fears of governmental authority which had been evident in Boston at the beginning of the century and which were now sweeping throughout the colonies.

Not only were citizens denied the right to vote or attend meetings, they also had only limited opportunities for participating through municipal officeholding. For by the mid-eighteenth century fewer men were holding office for longer periods of time. Whereas New York's governors appointed seventeen men to serve as mayor of New York City between 1683 and 1710, only three men held this post from 1747 to 1776. Likewise, New York City's sheriffs averaged two years in office during the late seventeenth and early eighteenth centuries, and yet by 1775 John Roberts was in his twenty-third year as city sheriff. New York's recorders averaged four to five years in office between 1683 and 1710, but Simeon Johnson occupied that post for thirty-two years between 1737 and 1769.[60] Only death or revolution would remove such long-standing incumbents as Johnson, Roberts, or Mayor Edward Holland from their positions within the stabilized municipal structure. The same situation existed in New Brunswick, where Thomas Farmar served seventeen years as mayor until his death in 1747, and his successor, James Hude, held the post for fifteen years until he died in 1762. William Ouke assumed the mayor's office after Hude's death and remained in that post for the rest of his life, dying in 1779 after forty-two years of continuous service as alderman, recorder, and finally mayor.[61] By 1770, then, life tenure seemed to be becoming a reality in fact if not in law.

Numerous municipal legislators also served lengthy terms as voters assigned control over local government to an aging body of perpetual magistrates. By 1773 Casper Shaffner was serving his twenty-first one-year term as a member of Lancaster's borough government, his colleague John Hopson had won election for the fifteenth time, and John Feltman was in his tenth term in office. Lancaster's borough officers in 1773 had won reelection an average of eight times as the townspeople mechanically reaffirmed their faith in the traditional incumbents at each annual election.[62] In Wilmington, Delaware, such continuity was less pronounced, but it was still evident, with the colonial borough officials averaging 5.3 years in office. By 1776 Wilmington's Watkins Crampton had won his twelfth annual term on the borough council, while Edward Dawes had served seventeen terms in borough government and John McKinley had held office for fifteen years.[63]

Meanwhile, in the province of New York the same pattern prevailed. New York City's council members of the period 1748 to 1773 averaged seven years in office, and during these same years Albany's councillors and aldermen averaged 5.3 terms on the council. During the mid-eighteenth century the voters of New York City's Out Ward elected Gerardus Stuyvesant as alderman thirty-two consecutive times, and there is no evidence that anyone ever ran against this perpetual member of New York City's governing body. Likewise, Abraham DePeyster and Francis Filkin both occupied their seats for twenty-five consecutive one-year terms, and Nicholas Roosevelt served twenty years on the common council. In Albany the patriarch Jacob Ten Eyck totaled twenty-two years as city lawmaker, John Bleecker held a seat on the municipal council for nineteen years, and Abraham Yates filled sixteen one-year terms in office.[64]

Stability, continuity, and order were the keynotes of municipal government during the last decades of the colonial era. The rulers of America's representative corporations were not necessarily aristocratic grandees, and the long-term leader Casper Shaffner was actually a simple dyer whose fortune ranked only slightly above the median for his town.[65] But whether they were modest dyers or wealthy merchants, these municipal magistrates remained in office year after year, suffering few electoral contests and rarely confronting partisan rivalry, for the idea of regular, consistent party clashes had not yet appeared on the municipal scene. Concord rather than competition remained the political ideal, and this emphasis on order and cooperation produced a series of stable municipal regimes. Revolutionary sentiments would eventually disrupt this relative calm, but during the 1760s and early 1770s Americans still aimed their political tirades primarily at Parliament and the royal authorities rather than at the humble municipal magistrates.

Not all urban Americans, however, sheepishly accepted the

established order and supported the status quo in municipal government. During the last decades of the colonial era, a few outspoken newspaper editors did occasionally level their biting rhetoric at the city fathers in an effort to render government more responsible to the governed. Such men feared irresponsible government authority, whether in the hands of Parliament, the church, the royal governor, or the municipal corporation. And each of these elements of the established order was to suffer attacks from blunt and bitter critics.

Among the sharpest opponents of episcopal authority and the Anglican establishment was William Livingston of New York City. Livingston's newspaper the *Independent Reflector* focused on the threat posed by bishops and Anglican clerics, but it did not ignore those other villains in positions of authority. Thus, during the mid-1750s Livingston expressed disdain for New York City's municipal government, writing facetiously of the "audacious Attempt of some evil disposed Persons to introduce into the Common Council men of Sense and Distinction." To reform the corporation by placing intelligent men in office, according to Livingston, would be a definite "Invasion of their ancient and undoubted Privileges." Moreover, the sharp-tongued editor devoted much space to exposing the questionable practices of the city council. According to the *Independent Reflector*, a five-man council committee which recommended the leasing of corporation property for an unusually low price included the son, brother-in-law, and son-in-law of those who desired to rent the property. For the council to "join in so iniquitous a Concession [was] utterly incredible," and any alderman who would favor such a plan should, in Livingston's opinion, "be considered as the Enemy of his Country and branded with eternal Reproach."[66]

Two decades later the New England–born editor of the *Pennsylvania Chronicle*, William Goddard, was to level similar attacks on the Philadelphia corporation. In a series of provocative broadsides printed in 1773, Goddard and a like-minded colleague exposed the evils of Philadelphia's municipal government and specifically lambasted a corporation scheme to build rent-producing market stalls in the center of an already congested thoroughfare. They viewed this market project as the last straw in a long series of municipal abuses, the final outrage committed by an autocratic corporation. Frustrated yet hopeful, these critics now issued their call to action, urging all to join them in a campaign for reform.

Underlying the criticism of Philadelphia's corporation was a fear of unchecked municipal power and incipient despotism. Thus William Goddard spoke out fervently against conceding to the corporation's market demands, arguing that such surrender would "add Strength to that Power which in some future Day may eradicate the Seeds of Liberty and destroy our Constitution."[67] An ally of Goddard's likewise spoke of "the successive means used by the Corporation to divest" the citizens "of part of their Rights and Privileges" and hinted of coming foul play when he accused the city government "of accumulating Wealth to give influence to their future Actions."[68] According to the reformers, the riches derived from proposed market rents would enter "a fund which will in time become dangerous to our constitution."[69] For such a treasury would offer despotic aldermen the financial means to achieve whatever nefarious ends they might desire.

In the face of this threat, Philadelphia's reformers advocated immediate revocation of the municipal charter. Thus Goddard urged his fellow Philadelphians to "lay the Ax to the Root" of the corporation "and apply . . . for a Dissolution of the Charter."[70] Another critic also proposed that the citizens seek forfeiture of "the Charter of the City by Reason of the Corporation's misuser of the Powers granted to them."[71] But no matter what the solution, action was necessary. Consequently one writer urged the reformers to continue their efforts, ensuring them that "good Men in our own Times as Well as Posterity will give Honor to the Men whose Intrepidity braved Oppression."[72]

Those who did dare to act were soon to be victorious, for a political revolution was about to disrupt the institutions of the American continent, and amid the onslaught Philadelphia's oligarchs would finally yield control. The Shippens and Chews, however, were not the only city fathers to feel the tremors of change. Magistrates in New York, New Jersey, and Virginia all stood at the threshold of a new era, an era of radical change in the nature of city government. The age of stable, consensual urban politics was finally coming to a close, and revolution and heightened political awareness would soon shatter the traditional relationship between governor and governed. In words similar to those spoken in Boston sixty years earlier men like Goddard and Livingston had expressed their suspicion of unlimited government authority and their belief in the necessity of strong checks on public power. During the next quarter-century they and their descendants would apply this rein to municipal corporations throughout America.

5 The Political Revolution

On a day in April 1775 a band of New England farmers and a corps of British infantrymen exchanged the first shots of the War for American Independence. Eight years of armed conflict would follow this encounter, conflict that would irrevocably sever the link between mother country and colony. Yet independence was not the only product of this imperial struggle. For as Americans established their new nation, they also set about to reorder the forms and procedures of government, carefully adapting past institutions to the political principles for which they were fighting. In an effort to ensure responsible, representative government, they wrote and rewrote constitutions, amended and revoked charters, invented an imaginative variety of checks and balances, and generally refurbished the framework of traditional politics. By the opening of the nineteenth century, the lawmakers of Massachusetts, Pennsylvania, and Virginia had created a fresh political structure suited to the republican ideals of Revolutionary America.

Among the institutions engulfed by this wave of structural reform was the municipal corporation. During the period 1775 through 1789 twenty-five towns along the Atlantic seaboard received charters of incorporation, and each document embodied provisions alien to the charters of an earlier age.[1] These revisions arose out of a new political context, a context of antiauthoritarian sentiment and libertarian concern. During the Revolutionary struggle, Americans had grown increasingly suspicious of governmental authority and increasingly jealous of their individual liberties. By the 1780s Thomas Jefferson was writing that "the people are the only censors of their governors," and "if once they become inattentive to the public affairs, ... Congress and assemblies, judges and governors shall all become wolves."[2] Men like Jefferson felt no sympathy for the unrestrained power of oligarchic magistrates or irresponsible aldermen. They feared and abhorred them. And this attitude transformed urban rule in America.

Chief among the changes in city government was a broadening of the opportunities for political participation. During the 1780s and 1790s the individual urban resident gained a greater voice in the making of municipal policy. In many of the colonial corporations, the average citizen had been at best a silent spectator viewing from afar the sport of urban politics. After the Revolution, however, many more joined in the game and exercised their power at the polls. Such a change was essential if America's urban dwellers were to check the much-feared despotism of their municipal rulers. For no talisman warded off the evil of tyranny so effectively as did the suffrage and the ballot box.

Indicative of this trend toward broader participation was the disappearance of the closed corporation. None of the municipal charters granted after 1775 created a governing body of life-tenure officers chosen by co-option. Instead, the councilmen in each of these new corporations were popularly elected and generally served terms ranging from one to three years. In a state like Virginia, this represented a radical departure from tradition. For before the Revolution not one of that state's municipal officers or any of its statutory commissioners were popularly elected. Yet in all six of the Virginia corporations established between 1779 and 1786 the choice of city officials rested with a broad electorate of householders or property owners. No longer would the men of Virginia submit to a municipal oligarchy of self-elected aldermen. Instead, they would now participate in a representative form of government, dependent on the will of the urban populace.

In two localities, however, there were short-lived attempts to preserve the custom of life tenure. Thus the post-Revolutionary charter of Georgetown, Maryland, specified that the city's popularly elected councillors would serve life terms, and not until 1797 did the Maryland legislature replace this anachronistic provision with one establishing biennial elections.[3] Farther north, proponents of municipal rule in Philadelphia drafted a new charter in 1783 which likewise provided that aldermen hold office "during their good behavior."[4] Reaction to this provision, however, was swift and sharp. Pennsylvania's legislature refused to sanction the charter, and at least one angry Philadelphian castigated the provision as being "in direct repugnance to the constitution."[5] When in 1789

Philadelphia did finally receive a new charter, it contained no such vestiges of past oligarchy. Rather, it created a representative body of limited-tenure aldermen and councillors consistent with the principles of Pennsylvania's Revolutionary constitution and the ideals of the young republic.[6]

Having discarded the practice of co-option, lawmakers confronted the question of who would constitute the municipal electorate. In defining this body, the Revolutionary charters again deviated from tradition. For in contrast with previous charters, none of the documents drafted after 1775 recognized the commercial status of master craftsman or freeman as a qualification for voting. Moreover, only one of these charters granted municipal aldermen the traditional power to expand or contract the electorate by selling or refusing to sell admission to an enfranchised status. The remaining twenty-four documents fixed definite voting requirements and thereby deprived city officers of any control over the franchise.[7]

In fifteen of the Revolutionary charters, such suffrage requirements limited the vote to those owning a specified amount of property or paying a certain level of taxes. For example, in Charleston, South Carolina, all white males who paid a tax equal to three shillings or more could vote in the city elections, and in Richmond, Virginia, this power belonged only to those possessing "movable or immovable property to the value of one hundred pounds." Likewise, only freeholders could vote for aldermen under Philadelphia's charter of 1789, and New Brunswick's patent of 1784 granted the municipal franchise solely to "freeholders and such of the inhabitants . . . as are by law qualified to vote for representatives in the general assembly."[8]

The nine remaining charters, however, were more liberal, bestowing the right to vote on virtually every resident who was not a vagabond or thief. Thus the new charters of Burlington and Perth Amboy, New Jersey, granted the suffrage to all residents "excepting such as during the late war have been guilty of licentious cruelties in plundering or murder contrary to the usages of civilized nations."[9] Carlisle and Reading, Pennsylvania, extended this same privilege to all "freeholders together with such . . . housekeepers within the said borough as shall have resided therein at least for the space of one whole year."[10] And in Alexandria, Winchester, and Fredericksburg, Virginia, "housekeepers" needed to live only three

months within the city to qualify for the right to vote.[11] Under none
of these Revolutionary charters did commercial rank entitle one to
the suffrage, and only a single charter of the 1780s authorized
borough aldermen to regulate admission to an enfranchised status.
For in the wake of America's revolution property and residency
had supplanted commerce and aldermanic consent as the chief
criteria for participation in the nation's urban politics.

These reforms in political structure seem to have enjoyed almost
universal support, arousing few complaints from devotees of
tradition. Yet beyond this there was little consensus on the subject
of the municipal corporation. For during the last quarter of the
eighteenth century, city government was a major topic of controversy, stirring the political passions of men from Boston to
Charleston. Throughout the nation concerned citizens debated the
merits of a variety of proposed or existing charters, subjecting the
institution of the municipal corporation to harsh scrutiny. From
these debates came further impetus for change, eventually resulting
in vital political reform.

Discussion of municipal government centered on two opposing
positions. On one side were those who emphasized the utility of the
municipal corporation in promoting trade, paving streets, and
preventing crime but who generally ignored the threat which
corporate rule might pose to the political rights and liberties of the
American people. In 1784-85 men of this outlook fought vigorously
for the incorporation of Boston, speaking forthrightly of the
administrative chaos which resulted from an inadequate town-
meeting government.[12] Meanwhile, in Philadelphia the political
faction which opposed Pennsylvania's radical constitution of 1776
likewise adopted the cause of municipal rule as a plank in its
partisan platform. Philadelphia's colonial corporation had ceased
to function during the Revolution, and now such Anti-Constitutionalists as Robert Morris and George Clymer endeavored to rid
the streets of accumulating rubbish, quell roving marauders, and
eliminate corruption by reestablishing municipal government.[13]

Opposing these men were those who spoke little of the practical
questions of markets, streets, or crime but instead focused their
rhetoric on the role municipal officers might play in undermining
republican government and instituting an aristocratic regime. Thus
Samuel Adams led those Bostonians who deplored changing the
town's constitution "from its present democratic plan, in order to

build up a new fabric approximating more nearly an aristocratical or monarchical government."[14] In Philadelphia John Smilie and William Finlay captained Pennsylvania's Constitutionalist faction in its struggle to defeat those who "designed incorporation to establish an aristocratic influence within the city."[15] And in Baltimore the local Republican club joined with the mechanic's society in a similar protest against the city's proposed charter of 1793-94.[16] All along the Atlantic seaboard men were expressing the same doubts about municipal rule, doubts arising from a supposed conflict between republican ideals and corporate government.

But these critics of the municipal corporation did more than simply harangue their enemies with cries of aristocracy and despotism. They also submitted the various city charters to a careful examination and specifically identified those features which appeared contrary to republican government and the preservation of liberty. By doing so, they focused attention on the need for additional reform and aroused public support for a program of structural renovation. Groups such as the Baltimore Republicans and the Pennsylvania Constitutionalists were not satisfied to simply discard the practice of co-option and the privileged status of freeman without making further changes in the framework of urban rule. They demanded broader reforms, and much discussion during the late eighteenth century centered on their proposals.

Most disquieting to critics of corporate rule was the concentration of legislative, executive, and judicial powers in a single body of municipal officers. Under the traditional corporate structure, the aldermen enacted and executed all ordinances and served as a court of justice when these laws were violated. The mayor was simply a member of the aldermanic board and possessed no veto power which might check its authority. In other words, there existed no sophisticated division of responsibility among competing branches of government, nor were there any relationships of countervailing power. Instead, the great bulk of authority rested in the hands of one group, a group many Americans viewed with fear and suspicion.

In the largest cities of the South, critics repeatedly cited the union of executive, legislative, and judicial power as a repugnant feature of municipal government. For example, a member of the South Carolina House of Representatives complained that Charleston's charter "blended the legislative, the judicial, and executive power in one body of men, and made them as despotic in Charleston as the grand Siguior is in Constantinople." According to this spokesman, Charleston's magistrates "have the power to massacre the inhabitants and burn the city" and "it is not by the freedom of our laws, but by the grace and goodness" of these aldermen "that we now exist and seem to enjoy a shadow of liberty."[17] In Baltimore this subject likewise commanded some attention, and Republican opponents of incorporation were themselves criticized for ignoring the problem of concentrated power. Thus one writer reminded Baltimore's reformers of the need for creating independent branches of government "to check hasty proceedings and . . . be a watch over each other." Reiterating the dangers of undispersed authority, he asked whether the townspeople would agree "to have all legislative and executive powers vested in the same body" when all who possess such inordinate powers "instantly become tyrants, oppressors and public plunderers."[18]

In the mid-Atlantic states of Pennsylvania and New York men were expressing similar objections. For example, John Smilie described the tyranny and plunder that resulted when "the whole power is . . . united in one body" and denounced such concentration as "contrary to every principle of justice and freedom." Quoting no less an authority than Montesquieu, Smilie predicted that "there would be an end of every thing were the same man or the same body . . . to exercise those three powers" of legislation, execution, and adjudication.[19] New York's State Council of Revision, led by Governor George Clinton, expressed similar sentiments when it vetoed a measure incorporating the city of Hudson. In its veto message, the council specifically attacked Hudson's charter for "blending the legislative, the executive, and the judicial departments" in a manner "destructive of the rights and liberties of the citizens . . . residing within the limits of the said city.[20] And in 1792 a state legislator questioned the extent of mayoral powers in New York City, arguing that "the accumulation of all powers, legislative, executive, and judiciary in the same hands . . . may justly be pronounced the definition of tyranny."[21]

New Englanders were equally fearful of the aldermen's extraordinary authority. Thus an opponent of corporate rule in Newport, Rhode Island, attacked that city's charter for subjecting "Six Thousand People . . . to the despotic Will of Eleven" aldermen "who are Legislators and Judges of their own Laws."[22] Likewise, in

Boston one critic asked whether the townspeople would wish "a court of ALDERMEN to be Law Makers, Justices of the Peace, Judges, Jury, and Executioners."[23] Another spoke similar sentiments, warning that "in all city corporations the Mayor, Aldermen and Recorder . . . make laws, judge of those laws, [and] execute those laws," and the consequence of this arrangement in Boston "will be absolute slavery."[24] To avoid such servitude political leaders from South Carolina to Massachusetts suggested either wholesale rejection of the municipal corporation as an instrument of urban rule or at least radical reform in the structure of city government.

Yet critics of corporate rule also sought to thwart municipal tyranny by broadening the channels for political participation. Thus they turned their pens against property qualifications which discriminated against the honest but poor laborer while favoring the wealthy and privileged. In areas with a tradition of town-meeting government, many further endeavored to preserve the right of each citizen to express his thoughts and grievances in common assembly. Consequently men like Samuel Adams fought vigorously against the introduction of indirect, representative government in an effort to maximize the political rights of the urban dweller.

Repeatedly New Englanders expressed their support for the town meeting and their belief that municipal government would entail serious restrictions on the rights of political participation. For example, one Bostonian warned his fellow townspeople against "resigning their LIBERTIES, and the freedom of debate [and] becoming subject to the control of a few men."[25] Others attributed the valiant and successful defeat of British tyranny to the independent spirit of the town meeting and questioned whether Bostonians should now abandon this defense against despotism. Thus a writer calling himself "Old Whackum" described the New England town as the breeding ground for America's revolution and claimed that without "public debates in Town Meeting the true knowledge of the unalienable rights and privileges of the people would not have been so universally disseminated."[26] Another critic of corporate rule likewise asserted that "those independent sentiments which we now possess, and which carried us through our opposition to Great Britain, we received from our Patriots when assembled in Town Meetings." In light of this he asked whether Boston's citizens would now be willing "to put the powers of taxation and legislation out of our own hands into those of the few."²⁷ To these various foes of municipal government, incorporation represented a scheme "to lodge in the hands of a few particular GENTLEMEN the power of the whole," and most Bostonians were determined to prevent such a shift.²⁸

In Newport, Rhode Island, proponents of town government also spoke against the limits corporate rule imposed on the rights of political participation. Thus one critic attacked the fiscal and appointive powers vested in the municipal aldermen, claiming that the city's inhabitants were "deprived of a Voice in the Disposition of their public Property . . . [and] a voice in the Appointment of their Officers." Under the aegis of the despised city charter, Newport's aldermen were collecting revenue without the direct consent of the electorate "and appropriating it without their Control."²⁹ No longer could the people of Newport participate in the frequent assemblies which had traditionally guided the destiny of the New England town. Instead they had become silent partners in local government, having yielded a major share of the decision-making authority to a body of city officials.

The people of New York City felt no such longings for the town meeting, but they did desire a charter amendment which would grant them a greater voice in their city's management. Throughout the 1780s and 1790s, New Yorkers agitated for the right to elect their mayor and recorder and sought to revoke the authority of the state Council of Appointment to choose such officials. Writing in 1785, one resident of the city argued that "the present mode of appointing the said officers" was "inconsistent with the principles of equal liberty" and asked that selection of the officials be "lodged in the hands of the people."³⁰ In 1791 another spoke of "that precious gem—*The right to elect those who are to govern*" and asked, "Who can judge better for the PEOPLE, than the people themselves?"³¹ Moreover, a New York legislator emphasized the impotence of the liberty-loving people of New York City when confronted by a state-appointed mayor. "How," he asked, "shall the freemen of this city call to account that man for an abuse of power?"³² According to this spokesman, the people exercised no check on the mayor's actions, and the result was irresponsible, despotic rule. If the people were actually to govern in New York City, they needed greater opportunities for participating in the political process and a larger say in governmental decisions.

In Philadelphia the debate over political participation centered not on questions of direct democracy or appointive officials but on suffrage requirements. Although the Pennsylvania state constitution granted the franchise to all male taxpayers, the proposed Philadelphia charter restricted the right to vote in city elections solely to freeholders. Thus John Smilie accused advocates of incorporation of attempting "to disfranchise three-fourths of the citizens of Philadelphia" in a manner "contrary to the great principles of liberty and justice which formerly influenced us to oppose the attempts of Great Britain."[33] Smilie's colleague in the Pennsylvania House of Representatives, Robert Whitehill, also denounced such voting restrictions as "directly opposite to the constitution" and repugnant to the ideal of no taxation without representation.[34] Still another commentator observed that as a result of incorporation "many mechanics and other respectable citizens would have been governed, and had their money disposed of, by a few great men, in the choice of whom they could have no vote." For under municipal rule even "the most respectable men in the city if not possessed of a freehold could neither give his suffrage for a common council man, nor be elected one himself."[35]

The men of Baltimore echoed this when they spoke of ensuring broad opportunities for political participation. For example, the "mechanical, republican, and carpenter's societies" opposed a charter provision which established an electoral college to select the city's aldermen and mayor, arguing that the general electorate alone "ought to have the right of judging the qualifications of its own representatives." Moreover, these same groups also challenged a clause requiring electoral college members to possess one thousand dollars in real or personal property. Explaining their objections to this qualification, the Jeffersonians and the mechanics asserted that "no restraint whatever ought to be imposed on the will of the people in the choice of that man (whether rich or poor) whom they believe best qualified to serve them."[36] Foremost in their minds was the need to eliminate obstacles to fulfillment of the popular will. For in Baltimore, unlike colonial Annapolis, the governed rather than the governors were to guide the course of the city's future.

The Republicans and the mechanics offered two additional criticisms which further reflected their concern for augmenting the power of the governed. First, they opposed a provision which required voice voting in city elections, a practice which in their minds left "the poor and middling class of people too open to influence from the rich." Second, this same coalition attacked a charter restriction which limited the city franchise solely to white inhabitants and thereby excluded "free negroes and people of colour . . . from any direct share in the making and administration of those laws by which themselves are to be governed." Like the class discrimination inherent in voice voting, this form of racial exclusion seemed "contrary to reason and good policy, to the spirit of equal liberty and our free constitution."[37] And it was this spirit of equality and liberty that critics in Baltimore, Philadelphia, Newport, and Boston were seeking to realize.

Moreover, critics of municipal charters were always conscious of the dangers posed by lengthy terms of office. No man should hold too much power for too long a time, and Americans of the 1780s and 1790s consequently sought to ensure frequent review by the electorate. The government of the new nation was to be a government responsible to the governed, and under such a system the sovereign people needed ample opportunity to evaluate their public servants. If the municipal structure was to develop in accord with the new modes of political thinking, municipal legislators would have to seek election at short intervals.

In various cities the populace was quick to demand this system of frequent elections. In 1794 Baltimore's Jeffersonians criticized the proposed charter for "rendering the elected independent of the electors for too long a time whereby inattentive . . . servants may be continued in office to the great injury of the people."[38] In both 1792 and 1796 reformers in Philadelphia petitioned the state legislature to amend the existing charter so that all council members would "be chosen for a term not exceeding three years" as compared with the existing practice of seven-year terms for members of the municipal upper house.[39] And in Boston proponents of municipal government had to remind those many who feared incipient aristocracy that "the people were to choose the makers of their By-Laws annually."[40] The colonial charters of America's representative corporations had generally provided for annual elections, and urban residents in Boston, Philadelphia, and Baltimore wanted to maintain this practice in order to keep a close watch on their lawmakers. By the 1780s and 1790s these townspeople fully realized that constant vigilance was a necessary safeguard against corrosive government tyranny.

The efforts of such skeptical citizens, moreover, were not

without consequence. For during the late eighteenth and early nineteenth centuries, reformers in Baltimore, Philadelphia, and elsewhere gradually attained the twin goals of limited aldermanic power and broad popular participation while also maintaining the municipal practice of frequent elections. By 1810 the municipal franchise in most cities extended to all white male taxpayers, and by 1840 even the taxpaying requirement had largely disappeared. In 1834 the people of New York City finally won the right to elect their own mayor as the voter's role in local government increased. Meanwhile, lawmakers were also solving the problem of concentrated power by adapting the federal government's three-branch scheme to the institutions of the municipal corporation. Thus the office of mayor slowly assumed a status independent of the board of aldermen, and this same board gradually lost its authority to exercise both legislative and judicial functions. The result was a representative, balanced government, checked by the rivalry of competing branches and the scrutiny of a broad electorate.

In Philadelphia this slow but steady transformation of the municipal structure was particularly evident. Whereas under the proposed charter of 1786 only freeholders could vote in both council and aldermanic contests, by 1789 John Smilie and his fellow Constitutionalists had succeeded in extending the suffrage in council elections to all resident taxpayers.[41] In 1796 a second round of reforms eliminated remaining freehold restrictions, limited all city legislators to three-year terms, and resolved the issue of concentrated power. From that date forward Philadelphia's aldermen would serve only as municipal judges, interpreting and applying the law but having no power of legislation. Responsibility for drafting and enacting ordinances would rest exclusively with a bicameral council which exercised no judicial authority.[42]

Elsewhere in the nation this trend toward dispersed power was also apparent. For example, during the 1790s New York City's aldermen gradually ceded their judicial functions to a newly created body of city judges and increasingly focused their attention on the business of legislation.[43] In 1806 Albany's corporation appointed a panel of municipal police justices and granted these magistrates certain judicial responsibilities previously performed by the city council.[44] Pittsburgh's charter of 1816 also reflected the prevalent concern for distributing governmental authority. Under the provisions of this charter the city aldermen would constitute a municipal judiciary, while the councillors alone drafted and enacted legislation. And in Cincinnati, the city charter of 1827 embodied this same scheme of divided authority.[45]

Baltimore's charter of 1796, in contrast, sought balance not through creating an independent judiciary but by strengthening the executive branch. Whereas in the traditional municipality the mayor had served simply as a chairman of the board of aldermen, under this charter Baltimore's executive enjoyed the extraordinary power to review and veto all council measures. Moreover, although the upper house of the council nominated candidates to fill appointive office, responsibility for selecting officials from among these nominees rested solely with the mayor. Thus Baltimore's innovative charter did not concentrate the lawmaking and appointive powers of municipal government in any single body but distributed them among the councillors and executive, thereby creating a relationship of countervailing power and checking the potential for tyranny.[46]

The charter of Nashville, Tennessee, granted in 1806, embodied certain features that further bolstered the power of the municipal executive. For under Nashville's charter, choice of the mayor rested not with the board of aldermen, as was the traditional practice, but with the general electorate. Consequently the mayor no longer was dependent on the legislative branch for his tenure in office but owed his position solely to the white male residents who composed the city's voting population. The result was a strong, independent executive capable of challenging and checking the formidable authority of aldermen and councillors.[47]

In the years after 1806 urban dwellers continued this work of adaptation and alteration. Yet at no later time did lawmakers introduce reforms equal in significance to those of the last quarter of the eighteenth century. For during this short span of years, leaders from Massachusetts to Georgia had repudiated such long-honored institutions as the closed corporation and discarded such traditional powers as the right of aldermen to control admission to the enfranchised status of freeman. In addition, an array of spokesmen had initiated a crusade to eliminate first the barriers limiting political participation and second the dangerous union of executive, legislative, and judicial authority within the municipal structure. Underlying these efforts was a fear and suspicion of irresponsible government power not subject to the check of a broad electorate or an interbranch rivalry. Thoughts of such unharnessed authority plagued the minds of Revolutionary Americans, and by 1800 they had taken serious steps to eliminate that evil.

This concern for authority and popular participation not only resulted in structural reforms but also produced vital changes in political practice. Chief among these was the development of competitive political parties. Before the Revolution, urban Americans viewed an opposition faction as necessary only in those extreme situations when the constituted authorities had exceeded their powers and acted in a manner dangerous to liberty. Opposition parties were medicine for an occasional malady within the government structure. They were not a tonic to be consumed regularly each year or two for the continuing good health of the political system. In fact, excessive doses of party rivalry could be hazardous to the well-being of the body politic and destructive to the public welfare. After the Revolution, however, tyranny and subversion seemed a constant threat. Hypersensitive to authoritarian evils, numerous Americans saw the specter of tyranny in the growing number of corporations, the increasing centralization of government authority, and the failure to create structural checks on officials and agencies. Amid this atmosphere of acute concern and sensitivity, the sheepish behavior so common in municipal politics during the colonial period could not long survive. A broad suffrage and a separation of powers alone would not eliminate the threat posed by suspect incumbents. The voters would have to exercise that suffrage effectively in support of opposition candidates in order to ensure the preservation of liberty and the perpetuation of popular rule.

During the 1790s many Americans did rally around opposition leaders as Jefferson's Republican party challenged the ruling Federalists. This rivalry arose primarily from conflicts within the national government, but by the close of the decade these parties were also vying for power on the municipal level. In New York City, the Federalists exercised control as they repeatedly captured a majority of votes in six of the seven wards.[48] Yet the Republicans fought with vehemence to secure power, attacking their foes as "despoilers of the rights of their fellow-citizens."[49] Meanwhile, in Philadelphia and Albany Republicans were also slandering Federalists and Federalists besmirching Republicans as urban Americans confronted the vigor and fury of local party rivalry.

During the first two decades of the nineteenth century, factional splits within the Republican party assumed greater significance. Thus, in New York City the faction known as Clintonians feuded with the faction labeled Burrites. And in Philadelphia a group supporting Governor Thomas McKean exchanged insults with a group opposing him. Yet the Republican-Federalist conflict continued to rage in Albany well into the second decade of the century. As late as 1817 the Albany common council consisted of twelve Federalists and eight Republicans, and the "pretty sharply contested" race of 1819 resulted in the selection of fourteen Federalists and eight Republicans.[50]

During the 1820s and 1830s, however, partisan conflict was to reach a new peak as the American municipality departed radically from the older tradition of unanimous, unchallenged elections. In the Albany city election of 1828, twenty supporters of President John Quincy Adams vied with eighteen men committed to Andrew Jackson for the twenty municipal council seats.[51] Moreover, such rivalry was not temporary as it had been in New York City during the 1730s. Instead, party slates opposed one another year after year as Jackson's Democrats again faced Adams's National Republicans in 1829, 1830, 1831, 1832, and 1833.[52] By the 1830s sharp partisan rivalry was a feature of life in Albany, New York City, Philadelphia, and the rest of America's municipalities.

It was this emergence of party politics that gave meaning to the formal, structural reforms of the late eighteenth and early nineteenth centuries. For with the development of party competition on the municipal level, America's broad electorate now had a choice at the polls. Urban voters no longer mechanically reelected incumbents by acclamation; instead they selected the candidate who best suited their desires. Just as competition rather than exclusion was becoming the ideal in the marketplace, so competitive party politics was becoming firmly intrenched at the polls. The regulated, restrictive, consensual communities of the past were yielding to the growing, surging, competitive urban hubs of the nineteenth century.

Gradually, then, during the late eighteenth and early nineteenth centuries, the municipal corporation was becoming a forum for political competition and debate, an arena in which citizens were more than merely spectators. A great number of urban residents could vote for political office, and an emerging party system ensured the citizen a choice at the polls. Further, by the beginning of the nineteenth century the corporations had abandoned past traditions of secrecy, allowing the citizen a greater knowledge of municipal affairs. As early as 1774 Norfolk's council had opened its doors to observers, and after the Revolution New York City's common council again permitted visitors to witness its meetings.[53] In 1796 the Pennsylvania legislature ordered that the doors of Philadelphia's council chamber "shall be open for the admission of all peaceable and orderly persons, who shall be desirous of being present at the discussion of any by-laws."[54] Seven years later the council of Bristol, Pennsylvania, ruled "that any well-behaved citizens could in the future attend the meetings of the borough council, that they might know what business is done, and to form a better judgment thereof."[55] For almost a century the municipal leaders of Philadelphia and Bristol had excluded the townspeople from these meetings which determined the future of their communities. In an era dedicated to government by the governed such barriers could not persist, and full information was made available to enlighten the urban voter.

Certain difficulties arose, however, when reform elements endeavored to repeal or renovate existing city charters, for lawmakers had traditionally viewed amendment or repeal as possible only with the consent of the city fathers. If the aldermen and councillors refused to surrender their powers or modify their procedures, neither Parliament, the crown, nor the provincial assemblies would dare to force such change. On the subject of charter amendment the word of the city fathers was final, and no body of reformers could obtain redress of their grievances through appeal to a higher authority.

Amid the tumult of post-Revolutionary America this roadblock could not long survive, for advocates of a broad suffrage and dispersed authority did not surrender when confronted with notions of inviolate charter compacts. Rather, they determined to destroy such a vital defense of the status quo and open the door to unlimited change. Their efforts formed a second act in the American drama of municipal revolution, an act that would end in reform triumph. By 1820 reformers would succeed in eliminating the requirement for aldermanic consent and clearly establish the state's right to unilaterally remold the framework of the municipal rule.

6   Reform and
             the Ascendancy
             of State Power

Throughout the eighteenth century, the doctrine of charter inviolability survived as a sacred relic in the pantheon of English Whiggery. The Stuarts had schemed to deprive Britain's boroughs of their ancient privileges, and so long as the memory of this outrage remained vivid in the Anglo-Saxon mind neither king nor Parliament dared to encroach upon the rights of a chartered corporation. In the East India Company debates of 1783 members of the House of Commons repeatedly asserted "that Parliament ought not, or could not, in any case whatever, violate a charter," for "charters . . . are not like other laws, repealable at the will of the Legislature."[1] On the opposite side of the Atlantic, John Smilie likewise observed in 1786 "that it is supported and believed by many . . . that charters once given cannot be revoked," and other Americans further testified to the contention that "once sealed the charter . . . is irrevocable, unalterable."[2] Thus in both Britain and America the corporate charter represented a sacred compact to be scrupulously honored by king and legislature. It was not simply an ordinary statute subject to unilateral amendment by the central authorities but was an inviolate grant of vested privilege.

This concept of corporate privilege would govern the thinking of Britain's lawmakers until the reforms of the 1830s, but among England's New World offspring another viewpoint was gaining favor. Many Americans were dissatisfied with existing municipal charters and found entrenched aldermen unresponsive to their pleas for reform. Consequently they turned to the state legislature for aid, demanding an unprecedented exercise of central authority over the municipal corporation. Confronting the state lawmakers was a choice between reform demands for dispersed power and a broad franchise and the aldermen's claims of vested rights and charter inviolability. Before the Revolution legislators would probably have sided with the aldermen. But America's struggle for independence had released a flood of enthusiasm for representative government, and no tradition of corporate privilege could now withstand this fresh onslaught of republican ideology. Thus when the desire for reform came into conflict with past doctrines of charter inviolability, it was the latter that necessarily yielded. America's revolution had wrought a radical change in priorities, elevating the political power of the governed to a place of national concern above the vested rights of those governing.

The net result of this change was to bolster state authority over local government, for when state lawmakers restructured the municipal framework, they clearly established the state's unlimited power over the organs of urban rule. No longer would the requirement of aldermanic consent stymie legislative efforts at reform. Instead, the municipal charter had now become an instrument of the central authorities, subject to their changing policies and demands.

The first challenge to the doctrine of charter inviolability came from those opposed to city government in Newport, Rhode Island. By 1786 a number of sources of discontent threatened the continued existence of the Newport corporation. Typifying the widespread prejudice against municipal corporations, one Newport man castigated cities as the sources "whence sprang the idea of prerogative and subordination, and the engine of royalty began to be employed."[3] Others attacked the charter for eliminating frequent town meetings and for concentrating legislative and judicial power in a single body of aldermen.[4] And on a less theoretical level, controversy raged over the respective rights of the Newport corporation and a Mr. Easton to some beach property.[5]

The result of this varied antipathy was a petition signed by 104 of the city's inhabitants calling on the state legislature to revoke "a mode of government novel, arbitrary, and altogether unfit for free republicans."[6] After a hasty review of the question, in March 1787 Rhode Island's lawmakers granted the petitioners' demands and put an end to corporate rule in Newport. The city aldermen had offered a "spirited defense of that charter of incorporation" and "of the rights and privileges of the citizens," but their efforts had been to no avail,[7] for the Rhode Island legislature had chosen to defy tradition and deprive Newport's citizens "of the many invaluable privileges guaranteed to them, in the most sacred manner by Charter."[8]

The following year Norfolk, Virginia, succumbed to a similar attack by reform-minded state legislators. Since 1736 a closed corporation of merchants had governed Norfolk, allowing the general populace no voice in the administration of the borough. Many of the aldermen had remained securely in power for decades, ruling complacently without fear of public animosity. For example, Robert Tucker had served thirty-one years as alderman, from 1736 to 1767, and Paul Loyall first assumed a seat on the borough council in 1757, rose to the rank of alderman in 1761, and still occupied that position in 1788.[9] Norfolk's corporation thus exemplified not the representative government lauded by Revolutionary theorists and pamphleteers but rule by a self-appointed clique.

Some townspeople, such as the obstreperous brothers John and Cornelius Calvert, found this form of government beyond the pale of legitimacy and launched a campaign "to overthrow our d——d despotic charter."[10] Among other charges they questioned the whereabouts of nine-years' interest due on a loan office certificate owned by the borough and specifically challenged the probity of the venerable oligarch Paul Loyall.[11] Finding little sympathy for reform among the corporation, the Calverts and like-minded colleagues laid their complaints before the Virginia legislature in the form of a petition "for making null and void the charter of this Borough."[12] The city fathers of Norfolk responded in turn with memorials "remonstrating against any Alteration in the Charter of this Borough" and instructed Norfolk's representative in the state legislature to support these remonstrances "in all . . . parts and admit of no Compromise."[13]

After two years of debate, the legislature acceded to reform sentiment and altered the "impolitic and unconstitutional . . . mode of electing common-councilmen for the borough of Norfolk." Henceforth those borough residents eligible to vote for the state House of Delegates would triennially elect a body known as the common council. The existing board of aldermen would no longer possess any legislative powers, but instead the popularly elected council would enjoy "the sole and exclusive right of passing by-laws, and taxing the freeholders and inhabitants of the said borough."[14] After 1788 no oligarchic clique would impose levies on the people of Norfolk, for in Virginia lawmakers were eager to realize the Revolutionary ideal of responsible, representative government.

Norfolk's leaders, however, continued their defense of the closed corporation, protesting the legislature's act as "unconstitutional and an infringement of the Rights of the Citizens of this Borough."[15] Moreover, the council and board of aldermen ordered the mayor to "take Counsel concerning the legality of the above Act."[16] But no further action resulted from this advice, and the oligarchs abandoned the struggle. The state had boldly chosen to restructure the charter of a municipal corporation, and their audacious break with tradition had succeeded.

Newport and Norfolk were relatively small cities, however, compared with the emerging metropolis of New York City and populous Philadelphia. These larger municipalities commanded the greatest attention among Americans, and consequently they would set the style for urban law. By hindsight, the examples of Newport and Norfolk appear merely as preludes to the dramatic climax of controversy in Philadelphia and New York.

Philadelphians grappled first with the question of the state's power to alter corporate charters. This subject had been a major issue in the bitter struggle between the state's Constitutionalist and Anti-Constitutionalist factions. During the 1780s the Constitutionalist-dominated state assembly had repealed the charter of the Bank of North America and violated the corporate rights of the College of Philadelphia. Proponents of these measures had argued consistently in favor of the supremacy of state authority over corporate privilege, whereas their anti-Contitutionalist foes had shuddered at the thought of excessive government intervention in the affairs of educational, religious, and business associations. Now Pennsylvania's legislators would again confront the subject of corporate sanctity and face the question of an association's rights in relation to the state government. The lawmakers would have to decide whether municipal charters were irrevocable compacts or merely legislative statutes expressing the alterable policy of the state.

The issue first arose before the state assembly in January 1792 during debate over a bill limiting the Philadelphia corporation's power to regulate public markets. Those favoring the measure were largely Western Pennsylvanians who attacked "the organization of the corporation and how dangerously the powers bestowed to them are vested."[17] They viewed the city charter "as a Constitution granted to the city of Philadelphia by the legislature of the state, a Constitution within their power to amend or repeal at pleasure."[18] Mr. Scott of Washington County insisted that "the corporation is in the hands of the Legislature . . . as clay in a potter's hands."[19]

Scott's colleague Albert Gallatin of Fayette County expressed his approval of "corporations established to superintend the application of certain property to certain particular uses" and argued that "their charters . . . should be held sacred." But he could not abide "corporations of another nature" and stated "that the legislature which granted charters of powers had a right to withdraw any portion of those powers at will."[20]

Opponents of the measure, in contrast, "contended that the act of incorporation was a charter . . . which could not be encroached upon, a contract that could not without breach of faith be impaired."[21] Mr. Fisher of the city of Philadelphia answered Scott's simile by asserting that municipal corporations "were no more in the power of the legislature . . . than an earthen utensil . . . baked and disposed of" was in the hands of the potter.[22] Moreover, he argued that "the corporation for any improper conduct was amenable to the Supreme Court" and not the legislature.[23] Remedies, Fisher believed, should proceed not from the assembly hall but from the courtroom.

When the proposal came to a vote, it passed the House but suffered a narrow defeat in the Senate. Voting on the measure adhered strictly to Constitutionalist and Anti-Constitutionalist party lines. Even though the bill would have aided eastern Pennsylvania farmers who supplied the Philadelphia markets, senators from the predominantly Anti-Constitutionalist eastern counties voted unanimously against passage, while those from the Constitutionalist strongholds in the west expressed unanimous approval.[24] It was a close escape, but for the moment Philadelphia's corporation was successful in staving off predators. Round one of the bout between state and city had ended in a corporate victory.

The municipality's success, however, was short-lived. For in 1793 a second round commenced as reformers launched a vigorous campaign to rid Philadelphia's municipal corporation of its archaic structure. Appealing to the state legislature for aid in their struggle against the recalcitrant city officers, these proponents of change asked for a unilateral alteration of the Philadelphia charter. The mayor and aldermen answered with cries of charter inviolability, and consequently the question of the state's power over the municipal corporation again formed the crux of controversy.

The struggle began with a "Memorial to the General Assembly" from a group of "citizens of the City of Philadelphia." According to the petitioners, "no government can be free if the legislative, executive and judiciary powers are vested in the same man . . . and . . . no government can be republican if artificial distinctions are recognized, and property alone is made the basis of representation." Despite the apparent wisdom of these truths, they said, the mayor, recorder, and aldermen of Philadelphia "act in a legislative, judicial and executive character" and "a great majority of the inhabitants of Philadelphia" are deprived by property restrictions of "the rights of man and the privileges of citizens." Moreover, "the term of years for which the Aldermen are chosen . . . is calculated to introduce arbitrary habits and decisions, and . . . the secrecy of the deliberations of the common council . . . is calculated to suppress information." To correct this situation the petitioners asked the legislature to "render the constitution of the city conformable to the constitution of the state and compatible with the equal rights and privileges of Freemen."[25]

Owing to disagreement between the Pennsylvania House and Senate, these reform demands remained caught in the state legislative process until December 1795. At that time a second series of memorials revived the issue, instigating further controversy over the rights of a municipality relative to the state. Again complaints centered on the questions of suffrage and separation of powers as reformers compared the ideals embodied in the state constitution with the anachronisms of the municipal body.[26]

But the Philadelphia city council was determined to ward off the forces of state intervention. Consequently it appointed a committee of five "to attend to the Progress of the . . . legislature on the Petition praying for an Alteration in the Acts incorporating the city," while the mayor asked the Speaker of the Pennsylvania House to permit counsel for the corporation to be heard in defense of the existing charter.[27] The Speaker granted this request, and the city's legal officer accordingly appeared before a House committee. Reminiscent of Fisher's contentions of 1792, the city's representative argued the inviolability of the Philadelphia charter, stating, according to one correspondent, that "you cannot dare to touch, alter, revise or amend the hallowed instrument." And to support his contentions he cited the example of Britain with its undisturbed municipal corporations.[28]

Reaction to these comments was loud and bitter. In response to the notion that "corporations are sacred," "A Free-Holder" expressed astonishment, noting in wonderment that anyone could believe "that the power that created cannot alter or amend." Further, he disgustedly dismissed the example of "the rotten corporation of England."[29] An article signed "Thousands" asked indignantly, "Must we tell our children and our children's children . . . that there exists a charter of incorporation, a roll of parchment, which possesses the wonderful, the magic power of binding them in chains forever?" This correspondent thought not and urged Philadelphians to discard "such puerile theories militating so directly against every principle of common sense."[30]

The great majority of the Pennsylvania legislature thought likewise, and in April 1796 the wishes of the reformers were fulfilled. Disregarding notions of charter sanctity, the state lawmakers granted city voting privileges to all Philadelphians eligible to elect members to the state House of Representatives. Moreover, they divided the executive, legislative, and judicial functions of the municipality among three distinct branches and thereby achieved a separation of powers.[31] The disputes of the 1780s were fading into memories, and old Anti-Constitutionalists were now less die-hard in their attitude toward charter inviolability. By 1796 they no longer formed an insurmountable barrier to reform and no longer blocked changes in the municipal structure. Thus the legislature was able to bring the structure of the Philadelphia corporation into conformity with the principles of the new nation and in the process assert the preeminent power of the state.

In New York City, however, theories of inviolable charters survived, hampering reform efforts throughout the latter part of the eighteenth century. The Federalist party controlled New York City during the 1790s, and Federalist magistrates were to rank among the staunchest defenders of municipal charter rights. New York's Jeffersonians, on the other hand, were to lead the forces dedicated to smashing ancient corporate privilege. In New York, then, as in Pennsylvania, the question of charter sanctity was to become entwined in the emerging political party conflicts.

Reform efforts began as early as 1790 when residents petitioned the legislature to alter the boundaries of New York City's seven aldermanic wards. The charter of 1730 had fixed these districts, and by the last decade of the century they varied in number of voters from 84 to 615.[32] At first the city council opposed alteration, but rather than confront the legislature in a showdown of power it

eventually consented to the change. Yet the very fact that petitioners had attempted to override the authority of the council by
appealing to the state legislature rankled many a friend of the city's
charter privileges. Thus "A Free Citizen" denounced "the glaring
and unconstitutional attack made on the CHARTER of this city by a
certain Junto" as a violation of the rights and privileges of the
citizens of New York.[33] Like many New Yorkers of the time this
"Free Citizen" preferred an anachronism to the prospect of state
meddling in local affairs.

During the 1790s, however, discontent increased as the Federalist council pursued a policy which severely limited the number
eligible to vote in city elections. Traditionally the suffrage in
corporation contests extended to all freemen and freeholders, with
freemen admitted at the discretion of the council. But during this
last decade of the eighteenth century, the council granted the
freeman status to relatively few, leaving the franchise primarily in
the hands of freeholders.[34] Those urging an expanded suffrage
denounced this tack and favored an opposite policy. For example,
William Livingston argued that any man born within the city of
New York is "by birthright a freeman" and claimed that a
"magistrate be deserving of the opprobrious epithet of tyrant
who . . . should exclude him from his inheritance by birth."[35] Thus
Livingston favored radical expansion of the electorate through
manipulation of the traditional status of freeman.

Others did not find this adaptation of old forms to new needs so
appealing. Rather, they favored a full-scale revision of the corporation and were not squeamish about the niceties of charter rights.
Chief among these men was the Jeffersonian leader James
Cheetham, who urged "that the elective franchise . . . be secured
. . . to all the regular inhabitants of the city with such rational and
liberal limitations as may be considered necessary for the public
good."[36] To achieve this end, the legislature would need to alter the
charter, and Cheetham did not hesitate in favoring state-imposed
amendments to that "sickly and effeminate" document.[37] For he
believed that a corporation was simply "the child and creature of
the state" and "the power by which it is created can always control,
amend or dissolve it."[38] Although he was skeptical of legislative
intervention detrimental to property, he contended that "no alteration of the charter" of the city "interferes with the enjoyment of
private property."[39] Rather, as Albert Gallatin had noted in 1792,

revision of municipal charters centered on questions of power and not land or money. And Cheetham believed that a change in the power structure of the city was absolutely necessary.

During the opening years of the new century, Cheetham and like-minded colleagues sought to realize this change through repeated appeals to the state legislature. Their first assault was on the perennial problem of malapportioned wards. By 1801 the boundaries again needed redrawing, and in March of that year residents of the seventh ward petitioned the legislature for this alteration. The House referred the petition to a committee which reported that "the inhabitants . . . must submit to their present inconveniencies" until the city council had asked for alteration, "as the committee are of opinion that the Legislature cannot, without violating the charter-rights of the city, add to the number of its wards but on application of the Corporation."[40] Thus for the moment charter rights had saved the city from the forays of state lawmakers.

By December 1802, however, Cheetham and the Jeffersonians had armed themselves for a second attack on the city's venerable but outdated charter. In a petition to the state legislature, these men asked for an extension of the franchise, an end to the practice of multiple voting by those possessing freeholds in more than one ward, ballot rather than voice voting, and an alteration of ward boundaries.[41] Accompanying this came a barrage of articles, diatribes, and protests asking, demanding, and pleading for charter revision. The *Morning Chronicle* warned against the notion of charter inviolability, noting that "a doctrine tending to raise a corporate body of this nature above legislative power and make it paramount, in effect, to the constitution . . . appears pregnant with calamity and danger."[42] Brockholst Livingston expressed similar sentiments when he argued that "it will be better to admit an absolute legislative control over all charters than the continuance of a practice pregnant with so many dangers."[43] And the Jeffersonian minority on the city council lauded "the correcting hand of legislative aid" as ensuring subservience "to the general good of all interested therein."[44]

Not all, however, believed in the benevolent omnipotence of the state's lawmakers, and these skeptics did not fail to express their opinion. "Caius" warned that "a combination has been formed to assassinate the Charter of the City for the purpose of promoting the cause of ruin, anarchy and confusion."[45] In a more temperate tone,

the *New-York Evening Post* reasoned that "the charter is a contract
between the government and the corporation which by mutual
agreement may be modeled as both the contracting parties may
think proper." Thus the *Post* asked, "Are not our privileges
impaired if the legislature assume their own will and pleasure
without the consent of the corporation?" And "if the legislature can
do this in one instance where are they to stop?"[46]

Despite such misgivings, the state legislature disregarded the
wishes of New York's city council and in March 1803 enacted a bill
to alter ward boundaries. The measure also received the approval
of New York's Council of Revision, but not without dissent. One of
the council's members, Justice James Kent, noted that "if the
alterations contained in the said bill can be made without the
consent of the corporation, the charter may . . . even be destroyed
whenever it shall seem meet to the Legislature." Thus Kent opposed
the measure, arguing that it "establishes a dangerous precedent . . .
which may lead to the destruction of all the chartered rights . . . of
this State."[47]

After passage of this redistricting bill, lawmakers and public
alike turned to the more significant question of expanded suffrage.
Faced with the prospect of franchise reform, one Federalist moaned
despairingly that "this great commercial city . . . is doomed to be
governed . . . by wretched rabble fashionably called the sovereign
people."[48] Others repeated the now well-worn doctrine that "charters ought to be held sacred, and that any alteration or amendment
unless in the mode prescribed in the instruments themselves is a
violation of *right*—an infringement of the fundamental principle of
the social compact."[49] But most agreed that the question of charter
rights had been settled by the bill altering the wards. As Colonel
Willett explained, "He had always been accustomed to consider the
Charter of this city in too sacred a light to be meddled with by the
Legislature, but . . . since they had begun with it, he confessed he
was for going further."[50] The legislature had violated the charter
once, and many felt little reluctance to do it again.

Accordingly, the state lawmakers enacted a second bill which
defined the electorate in terms of leaseholders and taxpayers rather
than freeholders and freemen. Moreover, this same measure eliminated the practices of multiple and voice voting, thereby reducing
the power of the wealthy to influence city elections.[51] In the future,
admission to the freeman's status would entitle the holder to neither

political nor commercial privileges. Rather, this ancient rank would survive simply as an honorary title granted periodically to visiting dignitaries.

Members of the Council of Revision, however, continued to express doubts about the rectitude of such a departure from tradition. When the bill for extending the franchise arrived in their hands in April 1804, they chose to veto the measure. Reciting an oft-used argument, the council stated simply that "charters of incorporation containing grants of personal and municipal privileges were not to be essentially affected without the consent of the parties concerned."[52] The House and Senate disagreed with the council, and theirs was the final say. By a two-thirds vote New York's legislators overruled the veto and settled the question.

During the next century, courts throughout the country reiterated this legislative determination in a stream of opinions fixing the spheres of state and local power. The triumphs over Philadelphia and New York City had added fresh territory to the state legislature's domain, and America's jurists did not shrink from sustaining the conquest. City officials continued to argue in defense of municipal privilege, and as late as 1838 the town fathers of New Brunswick were claiming that a unilateral charter amendment was "a nullity in as much as . . . it impairs the obligation of contracts."[53] Yet such opinions did not win much favor from the men on the bench. In a score of cases jurists recited the views of Gallatin and Cheetham, repeatedly describing the municipal corporation as an agent responsive to the state's mandate.

The United States Supreme Court first sanctioned this concept of the municipality in the Dartmouth College case of 1819. In his opinion Chief Justice John Marshall refused to extend contract-clause protection to municipal corporations, asserting that "if . . . incorporation be a grant of political power . . . the legislature of the State may act according to its own judgment" unrestrained by constitutional limitation.[54] Justice Bushrod Washington agreed, observing that "in respect to . . . cities . . . the legislature may, under proper limitations, change, modify, enlarge, or restrain them."[55] Justice Joseph Story detailed the nature of those proper limitations. Although Story was willing to allow state control of power relationships, like Gallatin and Cheetham he was dedicated to the protection of property. Thus he asserted that in respect to municipal corporations the state's power is not "so transcendent

that it may . . . take away the private property of the corporation."[56] In other words, Story agreed that the governmental powers
and structure of a municipality were clay to be modeled by the state
legislature, but that the city's nongovernmental holdings were
beyond the touch of outsiders.

This distinction between the municipality's "private" property
and its governmental functions survived as a rule of law throughout the remainder of the nineteenth century. But it offered only
mild consolation to harried city governments, for in subsequent
years state lawmakers would exercise their authority with a
vengeance, depriving municipalities of control over their own
police forces and waterworks and even supervising construction of
Philadelphia's city hall. During the late eighteenth and early
nineteenth centuries, America's city fathers had lost the battle for
ascendancy, and in the future they would suffer the misfortunes of
defeat.

The Changing
Nature of
Municipal Business

In 1800 Philadelphia's corporation financed construction of a city waterworks, Norfolk's common council ordered the recording of local health statistics, and New York City's aldermen debated whether to abandon their traditional control over bread prices.[1] Each of these actions was indicative of the changing nature of municipal business in the half-century following the American Revolution. For during these years numerous laws regulating prices and commercial activity gradually disappeared from the city ordinance books, while council agendas dedicated an ever increasing amount of time to the subjects of health, safety, streets, and waterworks. This trend had been apparent throughout the latter years of the colonial era, manifesting itself most significantly in the disappearance of the freeman's trade monopoly. Now, however, the rate of change accelerated as municipal government successfully adapted to improved technology, a rising standard of living, and Adam Smith's doctrine of free enterprise.

The objects of this change, the American cities, were no longer the crude little trading centers of 1700. By 1800 the largest of the metropolises, New York City and Philadelphia, had surpassed the 60,000 mark in population, and by 1820 both would have more than 100,000 inhabitants. New Yorkers were gradually moving northward from the tip of Manhattan Island, and Philadelphia's population was sprawling westward from the Delaware River toward the Schuykill. Moreover, as Philadelphians moved outward from the city center, they began to spill over into new zones of population beyond the corporation limits. These satellite settlements grew rapidly during the early nineteenth century so that by 1820 a cluster of separate towns and municipalities surrounded the original city of Philadelphia.

Farther west, Americans were establishing cities in areas only recently surrendered by the Indians. Pittsburgh was fast becoming the chief urban center of western Pennsylvania, and as early as 1820 Cincinnati, Ohio, could claim more than 9,000 inhabitants. Saint Louis dominated the commerce of the upper Mississippi and had 4,600 residents by the close of the second decade of the nineteenth century. And guarding the mouth of the great Mississippi basin was the largest city in the west, New Orleans, with a population of 27,000 in 1820. Thus throughout western America urban centers were rapidly expanding in both wealth and numbers as the nation exploited the vast resources of the lands beyond the Appalachians.

Though America's cities had grown considerably in both population and wealth during the eighteenth century, in some ways they had changed only slightly. They were larger, with more people, more paved streets, more elegant buildings, more ships in the harbor, and more wagons in the market. But the American city, unlike its English couterpart, was only beginning to feel the impact of the industrial factory system. As late as 1820 America's urban areas remained primarily centers of trade and handicraft manufacturing rather than mill or factory towns. Moreover, innovations in transportation had not yet confronted the urban world with startling new problems and vast new opportunities. The American city was still a walking city as it had been in 1700, with horse-drawn transportation used primarily for moving freight. As yet it had not experienced the railroad or the streetcar, and the overwhelming majority of ships in its harbors were still masted schooners and sailing packets rather than newfangled steamboats. Water remained the cheapest and easiest form of transportation, and country roads were hardly better than they had been a century before. Thus urban areas in 1800 as in 1700 hugged the navigable waters of the Atlantic coast and the inland rivers, and along these waters sailed the commerce in agricultural goods which still constituted the American city's economic mainstay.

In 1800, then, America's cities were no longer the rude outposts of 1700 but were rapidly expanding centers of trade and commerce with a population demanding new services and new approaches to municipal rule. The modes of transportation and manufacturing in America had not yet changed radically in nature, but the people's expectations were already on the rise. Urban Americans now demanded a systematic approach to the problem of disease, a more sophisticated system of public works, an end to some of the traditional strictures on commerce, and a policy dedicated to greater entrepreneurial liberty. They expected the municipal corporation to rearrange its priorities, and during the half-century following the American Revolution the city fathers heeded their demands.

This change in attitude was apparent in the comments of those who had now begun to challenge the municipality's role as commercial promoter and regulator. As early as the 1780s, one Philadelphian observed that "the experience of England has not manifested that trade or industry are promoted by the charters of her cities or boroughs." To support his argument he mentioned the rapid growth of such "divers unincorporated towns as Manchester, Birmingham, &c." and cited the economic prosperity which these cities enjoyed owing to an absence of municipal rule.[2] During this same decade, another Pennsylvanian likewise spoke critically of "the spirit of restraint upon the competition of . . . manufacturers" which resulted from excessive municipal regulation.[3] And yet another warned that "our liberty will be lessened and our trade cramped and fettered by an act of incorporation."[4] In each of these cases the message was the same. All three stated simply and clearly that the burdens of municipal regulation far outweighed the economic benefits which might accrue from the establishment of city government.

Similar comments appeared in 1792 during the Pennsylvania Assembly debates over market regulation in Philadelphia. In these debates, political leaders began to challenge the long-accepted belief in government regulation of the economy. Spokesmen no longer depicted the municipal authorities as expert mechanics capable of creating a finely tuned equity but described them as harmful meddlers gumming up the natural market mechanism. New ideas were emanating from the Edinburgh study of Adam Smith, and these fresh notions were strongly influencing the American concept of the municipal corporation.

Leading the forces opposed to municipal regulation was the Pennsylvania state legislator and future secretary of the treasury Albert Gallatin. In a speech before the legislature, Representative Gallatin deviated markedly from traditional thinking when he attacked those "tyrannical and absurd" ordinances which banned the practice of forestalling. He insisted that "every law which puts a restriction on trade instead of being attended with beneficial [ends] would produce a contrary effect." Reading from Adam Smith's *Wealth of Nations*, Gallatin told his colleagues that "self-interest without the interference of legislatures or corporations...could regulate the concerns of trade much better than any regulations" imposed by aldermen and councillors. Restrictions on trade were baneful to progress, and "all such laws will tend to impoverish the country and starve towns."[5]

At the same time, an anonymous correspondent in one of Philadelphia's newspapers was likewise arguing in favor of unfettered market trading. This writer believed that all past efforts "to prevent engrossing, forestalling, or too high a price being charged" had been fruitless and "not often attended with any beneficial effects." Instead, "it will almost invariably be found that those commodities which are ... left entirely to the enterprising spirit of the dealers ... are sold on fairer terms than those which have been regulated by the combined wisdom of our sapient Legislators." Closing with a quotation from Lord Bacon, this correspondent proposed that "if Government be desirous of trade, there cannot be a better method than to let the practisers thereof follow it in their own way."[6]

Later in the decade others joined in this growing chorus of dissent. For example, a group favoring reform of Philadelphia's charter castigated the "peculiarly obnoxious" authority of "the common council to prescribe prices of labour and regulate particular occupations."[7] Moreover, in Baltimore the Jeffersonian faction launched a similar assault on the power of the municipality to fix wharfage rates, denouncing this power as "productive of a most pernicious interference with the rights of private property."[8] For each of these critics questions of commercial chicanery and equitable dealing were no longer of chief concern. Instead, such men as Gallatin and the Baltimore Republicans placed preeminent emphasis on freedom of enterprise and the rights of economic liberty.

Such views, moreover, were not without practical consequence. For during the post-Revolutionary era city fathers responded to a surging wave of criticism and abdicated the significant regulatory task of price-fixing. Whereas before the Revolution corporation officials determined the cost of all commodities sold in the public markets of Albany and New York City, after 1800 no such comprehensive program of price regulation existed in any American municipality. In some cities such as Baltimore and New Haven, the municipal fathers did not even choose to regulate the price of bread. But in the municipalities of New London, Albany, New York City, Pittsburgh, Charleston, and Savannah, traditional restrictions concerning the sale of breadstuffs persisted throughout the 1780s and 1790s.

Such restrictions did not, however, survive the early decades of the nineteenth century, for during these years angry bakers revolted against the restraints upon their trade and succeeded in eliminating long-standing strictures which stifled their efforts to earn a living. In the past, bakers had protested the actions of municipal officials, but unlike the butchers of the 1760s they had not demanded an end to the practice of municipal price-fixing. Rather, they had sought only revisions and adjustments in the city's price schedules or quality standards. Now they favored a more drastic change and urged the introduction of a free, unfettered market in baked goods. By the mid-nineteenth century they had largely achieved this end as corporation officials in New York City, Albany, and Philadelphia no longer required bakers to sell loaves at one or two pence a pound. Instead, determination of price rested solely with the buyer and seller.

Typifying the struggle to eliminate price-fixing was the conflict between bakers and aldermen in New York City. Bakers were bitter about the municipality's power to limit their profits, and in 1800 New York's corporation temporarily acceded to these attacks and repealed all ordinances governing the cost of bread.[9] One year later, however, the aldermen and councillors reconsidered the issue and reenacted a schedule of bread prices.[10] Enraged at this action, the bakers then voted to shut down their ovens until the city fathers again repealed the measure. According to the striking producers and their allies, it was "impolitic" and "arbitrary" to "limit a set of men to a certain price of a certain quantity of any article,"[11] and by means of a strike the baking trade sought to impose this view on the people of New York.

Many New Yorkers, however, strongly resented the bakers' attempt to starve the city into submission. They castigated the strike as "a combination at once illegal and inhumane" and complained that the public had not received sufficient warning of the action. The bakers had not given "even one day's notice to the inhabitants" or afforded them "an opportunity of providing themselves with a supply of bread or of flour" to tide them through the period of the strike. Instead, the baking trade had arrogantly disregarded its duty to the public, and consequently its act merited "the contempt of every good citizen."[12]

Others warned of the future inequities which would result from a suspension of price restrictions. If there were no form of municipal regulation, one New Yorker concluded, the bakers "under the influence of self-interest . . . would think of accommodating themselves before they accommodated the poor."[13] Another quoted an article which described the consequences of regulatory neglect in Baltimore. According to the report, Baltimore's bakers misrepresented the weight of loaves, overcharged the customer, and sold a low-quality bread "which appeared to be made of condemned flour, or at best flour not of a better quality." The victims of such perfidy, moreover, were those least capable of protecting themselves. For the "profits of the bakers have been drawn not from the more wealthy classes of our citizens, but from those classes that have not the ability . . . for procuring flour and baking their own bread."[14] Thus in the absence of regulation the weak stood vulnerable to the strong and greedy, and this was a situation many New Yorkers wished to avoid.

By the close of 1801, those favoring municipal price-fixing had squelched the bakers' cause. During the strike a group of enterprising businessmen established the scab-operated New York Bread Company, and this organization soon emasculated efforts to force repeal of the city's regulatory ordinances.[15] Admitting defeat, the bakers agreed to accept the corporation's price schedule, which specifically fixed profits at twenty-eight shillings for every 250 pounds of flour used.[16] Thus the strike had achieved nothing. The corporation remained in control of pricing, and the bakers remained subservient to the municipal will.

During the next two decades, however, New York's system of municipal price regulation gradually collapsed. By 1815 the corporation was failing to enforce the authorized schedule of bread prices, and a writer in the *New-York Evening Post* claimed that he had not "noticed the regulation of this important article of life by the Chamberlain of our city for some months past."[17] In response to such critical comments, New York's city officials briefly resumed their supervision of bread prices, but dedication to the ancient ideal of economic regulation was obviously on the decline.[18]

Amid this changed atmosphere, New York's bakers in 1821

launched a second assault on government price-fixing and petitioned the city council "that all restrictions on the Sale and manufacture of Bread may be taken off."[19] Again foes of municipal interference exercised their pens, describing the baker as a "slave of corporation dictation" and defending the right of each buyer and seller to bargain freely. Thus one correspondent wondered why the corporation should have any right to interfere when "a baker makes bread to suit his customers . . . and for a sum . . . satisfactory to both the contracting parties." This same critic further argued that such meddlesome behavior was not only arbitrary but also detrimental to the production of high-quality, low-cost bread. Accordingly he predicted that "bread will be better in quality and greater in quantity for a given price without any restriction whatever." For in this man's opinion "all the restriction that can be devised will only trammel the subject" and undermine his ability to produce.[20]

New York's municipal leaders responded to these sentiments with a compromise solution. In December 1821 the common council repealed all previous ordinances regulating the sale of baked goods but enacted a new measure which required bread to be sold in standard one-, two-, three-, or four-pound loaves.[21] Such a requirement would lessen the possibility of fraudulent dealing and provide some protection for the consumer, but it would leave determination of price levels to the contracting parties. Thus the municipal corporation abdicated an unpopular portion of its authority over commercial transactions, but it refused to entirely abandon trade regulation.

Elsewhere municipal leaders were forced to take similar action. For example, Albany's corporation finally discarded the regulation of bread prices in 1820 after suffering through a bakers' strike and years of intermittent conflict.[22] In place of past ordinances, the Albany common council, like its counterpart in New York City, enacted a measure requiring all loaves to conform to a standard size.[23] Philadelphia's corporation enforced a similar law after the repeal of municipal price-fixing in 1797, and the councillors of Baltimore imposed this same restriction during the early nineteenth century.[24] Thus America's municipalities had discarded mandatory price schedules, but the regulation of weights and measures persisted.

The municipal system of market regulation also appeared to be collapsing during these years as city officials failed to enforce existing ordinances and traders took advantage of government indifference. In 1801 a group of New York City butchers complained that some of their colleagues "are in the constant practice of forestalling the market by riding into the country to meet the droves of cattle coming to the New York markets."[25] Two years later a committee of the common council studied the situation and found the complaint to be justified. According to the committee's report, "the laws against forestallers have been for a great length of time but partially executed, if not totally neglected, whereby the prices of provisions are much enhanced."[26] A leading observer of New York City's markets during the nineteenth century reported that enforcement varied from year to year, with some municipal officials "being . . . too stringent" while others were "tinctured too strongly of free trade to be suitable for the protection of the citizens."[27] Inconsistency, misunderstanding, and indecision seemed to prevail throughout this period as faith in past dogmas of economic control gradually dwindled.

During the first two decades of the century, market offenses continued to increase as a set of unlicensed butchers known as "shinners" or "shirks" began to populate the marketplaces of Philadelphia and New York City.[28] In nineteenth-century Philadelphia farmers could sell their own produce in a reserved section of the market house without paying any rent to the city, and in New York authorities demanded only a small fee from country people. The shirk butchers took advantage of this arrangement by posing as farmers and offering their meat in the low-rent area designated for rural producers. Meanwhile, municipal leaders continued to require licensed butchers to lease market stalls and pay substantial sums into the city treasuries. Thus the unlicensed interlopers enjoyed a low overhead, while the licensed butchers dug deep into their pockets in order to pay the charges demanded by municipal authorities.

This situation aroused the anger of licensed butchers, and as early as 1811 Philadelphia's legal operators petitioned the city council for action against shinners and shirks.[29] In an effort to correct the abuse, Philadelphia's council in 1815 asked the state legislature for permission to require rent from farmers using the markets as well as from city residents. Philadelphia's attempt failed, however, and New York City's leaders were no more successful in dealing with the interlopers.[30] In 1818, a committee of the New York City common council reported that virtually all of the supposed country people in the market "are Butchers or Hucksters in disguise." In fact, according to the committee, "it is a rare thing to see a farmer in the market with meats &c. of his own raising."[31]

While licensed butchers suffered from the competition of illegal shirks, they also complained of the increasingly heavy payments demanded for market stalls. In order to force a reduction in rents, New York City's butchers in 1821 agreed not to bid on any of the stalls offered by the city at the newly constructed Fulton Market. When one part-time butcher did lease a stall, his colleagues waylaid him, dragged him to the river, and tossed him off the end of the nearest dock. Finally the city and the butchers agreed on a compromise, and the municipality was able to lease the stalls. The lessees, however, soon found themselves unable to pay the exorbitant rents demanded, and the city retaliated by throwing them into jail. By the 1820s, then, the city was imprisoning licensed butchers while unlicensed shirks plied their trade and avoided heavy municipal exactions.[32]

With stall rents rising the number of illegal operators also mounted, and they became increasingly bold. In the 1820s unlicensed butchers no longer limited their sales to the public markets but began vending meat wherever they wished. From the middle of the seventeenth century onward, America's municipal corporations had required vendors to sell all meat in the public markets during a certain period of hours and according to certain fixed rules. Yet by 1823 speculators in the Bowery section of New York City were "purchasing hogs, sheep, and calves, and offering them for sale there, and other places" rather than being "compelled to attend the regular and legal markets."[33] In 1829 a rebellious butcher refused to pay the high rent demanded by the city for a market stall and instead opened New York City's first private meat shop,[34] and others soon followed his example as the public markets slowly declined in commercial importance.

Meanwhile, in Philadelphia a free market was also developing in fact if not in law. In 1819 a group of "Stall-holders in the High Street Markets" asked the Philadelphia city council to crack down on butchers who failed to lease municipal market stalls but instead "retail Beef from Carts and temporary Stalls."[35] Yet law-abiding butchers enjoyed no relief during the following decade, and in 1829 the lessees of market stalls in Philadelphia were still complaining about "the practice of selling meats from carts, wagons, and other vehicles and temporary stands in the streets, and of hawking it about from house to house."[36] In Philadelphia as in New York City the ancient market monopoly was gradually disintegrating as traders realized that they could earn greater profits under a system of free, unrestricted commerce than under the traditional system of municipal control.

This free-trade attitude also influenced those traditional foes of municipal regulation, the independent New Englanders. In the 1780s the newly created corporation of New Haven, Connecticut, established a public market and forbade the sale of meat and vegetables elsewhere during the morning hours. Yet according to Reverend Timothy Dwight of New Haven, "several respectable citizens opposed the establishment so strenuously and perserveringly as finally to destroy most of its good effects." By 1810 Dwight found it necessary to deplore the absence of market restrictions in the city and contended that "the greatest evil which the inhabitants suffer is the want of a regular system." He concluded that "there is something very remarkable in the hostility of the New England people to a regular market" and cited this persistent hostility as "a striking example ... of the power of habitual prejudice."[37] Moreover, such habitual prejudice continued to govern the attitudes of New Englanders, and in 1826 New Haven's city council repealed its market ordinance and officially abandoned its attempts to create a traditional municipal market.

From New England to Georgia the traditional concern for a regulated and restricted urban economy was gradually disappearing. Butchers, bakers, and market vendors were tossing off the restraints of the past, and municipal officials were slowly adjusting to a growing number of complaints and criticisms. The eminent jurist James Kent attributed these developments "to the increasing knowledge of the ... science of political economy and a sense of the folly of undertaking to regulate prices."[38] Thus Kent perceived changes in the nature of economic thought as what had formerly appeared sensible came to seem foolish. The ideological context of American life was changing, and the ideal of regulated concord was yielding to an ideal of open competition. The result would be an increasing interest in free trade and a decline in the importance of municipal regulatory measures.

During these same years, such promotive features as the commercial fairs also felt the effect of this change. Municipal leaders of the colonial era had traditionally used the fairs as a means for attracting trade to the community and promoting local business. In Burlington, New Jersey, the municipal corporation sought to develop the borough as a center of livestock sales, and consequently at fair time "that Corporation . . . provided and set apart commodious Lots of Ground . . . free of Charge for the Reception of such Beasts." Moreover, the Burlington city fathers endeavored to attract textile merchants to their community and thus invited "all Persons to bring to the said Fairs all kinds of Linen and Woollen Manufacturers . . . and four convenient Stalls will be assigned them Gratis."[39] During fair days the municipal authorities traditionally would not enforce exclusionary restrictions, and trade would be free and open with the merchandise of a variety of out-of-town peddlers and craftsmen spread before the townspeople.

By the time of the American Revolution, however, municipal officials generally ignored exclusionary ordinances, and city shops carried a wide variety of mechandise. Consequently, the fairs were not of such economic importance as earlier, and by the 1770s some regarded these gatherings as a definite nuisance. In 1773 the borough council of Bristol, Pennsylvania, concluded that the municipal fair "is a real evil and calls for redress" because of the "debauchery, idleness and drunkenness, consequent on the meeting of the lowest people together."[40] Two years later the Philadelphia corporation agreed that the fairs "have since the great Increase of Stores and Shops for the Sale of every species of Merchandise, been found not only useless, but . . . have become real Nuisances." According to Philadelphia's councilmen, the fairs "tend to debauch the Morals of the people, and to facilitate the Commission of Thefts and other Offences within the said City." Philadelphia's municipal fathers thus asked the provincial government to repeal the charter provision which required the holding of these shamefully immoral events.[41]

During the post-Revolutionary period the state legislatures finally responded to such requests. Philadelphia's new charter of 1789 did not provide for commercial fairs, and state lawmakers discontinued the Bristol borough fair in 1796 and the fairs of Lancaster, York, and Harrisburg in 1816.[42] Likewise in New Jersey the post-Revolutionary charters of the 1780s did not authorize the holding of municipal fairs. In the mid-eighteenth century the spring and autumn fairs in Lancaster had been a major source of municipal revenue and a focus of social cavorting and festivities, but by the second decade of the nineteenth century this ancient commercial institution was virtually extinct.

Such changes, however, were of secondary importance compared with the rapidly expanding programs for the preservation of urban health, the construction of streets and waterworks, and the beautification of the city. These concerns were to become the new focus of municipal attention as the urban populace demanded a cleaner, a healthier, and a more beautiful environment. No longer would consideration of markets, wharves, and livestock pounds dominate discussion in city council meetings. Instead hospitals, gutters, reservoirs, and parks would now be the center of the municipality's expanding endeavors.

In no field did the municipal corporation achieve greater progress during this period than in public health. Before the Revolution America's cities had engaged only in rudimentary schemes for eradicating disease and providing permanent nursing facilities. During the 1790s, however, the tragedy of yellow fever forced municipal leaders to initiate an unprecedented program for bettering urban health conditions. In one summer the fever killed one-eighth of the population of Philadelphia and one out of every fourteen persons in the smaller borough of Harrisburg, Pennsylvania.[43] To prevent a repetition of such slaughter, cities throughout America now decided to take action.

To guide this urban offensive against disease, various municipalities established and maintained local boards of health. The borough of Wilmington, Deleware, organized such a board in 1793, as did New Haven, Connecticut, in 1795 and Savannah, Georgia, in 1804.[44] Moreover, Philadelphia's corporation appointed members to a state-created board of health inspectors from 1794 onward, and New York City financed a similar commission beginning in 1796.[45] Each of these bodies quickly set about to rid their city of disease-breeding filth and to protect the populace from contagion. For example, New York's commission, together with some members of the common council, investigated "the causes of the pestilential disease which has lately prevailed in this city" and issued a list of twenty-four means for preventing the recurrence of such sickness.[46] New Haven's board also reviewed the dangers threatening urban health and obtained permission from the state legislature to quarantine foreign ships entering the city's port.[47] And Philadelphia's board likewise attempted to combat pestilence by recommending a program of street cleaning and quarantine.[48]

Responding to such suggestions, city fathers enacted an increasing number of ordinances aimed at preserving the public health. For example, in 1806 the aldermen of Charleston, South Carolina, decreed "that the preservation of health ... depends on a strict regard to cleanliness" and consequently ordered the removal of "all putrid substances, by which the air shall or may be impregnated with foul and noxious effluvia."[49] And in 1808 Albany's city council justified its street maintenance program by arguing that "it is requisite for the preservation of the health of the citizens, that the streets and lanes in the city be swept and kept clean."[50] Ten years later the councillors of Norfolk expressed a similar concern, ordering the city inspector to cause all "putrid or unsound substance ... to be destroyed by casting them into the stream of Elizabeth river or ... in such other manner as in their judgment may most effectually secure the public health."[51] And the aldermen and councillors of New York City enacted a virtually identical ordinance requiring the disposal of such rubbish in either the Hudson or the East River.[52] Throughout America municipal leaders were attempting to cleanse the cities of filth and create a safer environment. After centuries of plague and pestilence, the municipal corporation was finally applying its resources to a full-scale campaign against disease.

In a further effort to protect the public health, some municipalities also financed and maintained permanent nursing facilities. Thus in 1794 New York City's corporation established Bellevue Hospital for the care of those suffering from contagious diseases, and during this same year Pennsylvania's legislature authorized the aldermen of Philadelphia to "purchase some convenient lot of ground ... for the purpose of erecting and establishing thereon a public hospital."[53] In Baltimore the city health commissioners also operated a permanent nursing facility, and the corporation of Charleston maintained an institution staffed by a surgeon and a corps of nurses.[54] Later in the nineteenth century numerous other cities would establish public nursing facilities, but as early as 1800 such municipalities as New York City and Charleston were already maintaining centers to care for the sick and ailing.

Urban residents during the early nineteenth century were very conscious of the possible dangers to their health and actively demanded a continuation of municipal efforts. In 1802 "the Owners and Occupiers of the Houses and Property in Moravian Alley" petitioned the city of Philadelphia to repave their alley because water stood "stagnant in the . . . Holes to the great Danger of the Health of the neighborhood."[55] Likewise, residents in the Cherry Street area of Philadelphia asked for municipal action when they complained of stagnant water in an alley "which being often disturbed by Swine imparts a smell not merely offensive but at times almost intolerable and very dangerous to health."[56] And the inhabitants of Philadelphia's North Sixth Street described how they had "suffered great losses through the great accumulation of Water . . . that . . . frequently filled their Cellars" and created a situation "dangerous to the Health of the Citizens of the Neighborhood!"[57] They too asked for paving and gutters as a means of warding off disease and ensuring a better and safer way of life.

This concern for public health and safety also aroused unprecedented interest in the dangers arising from an inadequate and unwholesome water supply. Americans had seen too many people die owing to the supposedly harmful effects of noxious vapors from brackish wells and the inability to wash and cleanse streets. They had also seen too many homes destroyed and lives lost in fires that could have been extinguished had an adequate water supply existed. Urban dwellers were now hopeful of victory over these past terrors, and aldermen, councillors, physicians, and firefighters were all on the alert against future epidemics or disasters. But neither the boards of health nor the fire departments could achieve their goals if the cities were without a safe and abundant source of water. Thus a new and better system of water supply was necessary in order to quench the thirst of the expanding populace and provide for the health and safety of urban America.

During the colonial era, America's municipal corporations had occasionally constructed wells, but their water was often brackish and unfit for human consumption. In 1749 the Swedish traveler Peter Kalm noted that the water from Albany's wells "had a kind of acid taste which was very disagreeable" and reported that only "those who are less delicate in this point make use of the water from the wells" in New York City.[58] As early as 1760 a group of residents of Jonker Street in Albany organized a scheme "for bringing water in Pipes from the hills" and asked the Albany corporation to approve their plan.[59] New York City's municipal corporation failed to complete a similar project during the early 1770s, and in 1772 a Lancaster tanner asked permission to lay a pipe from a spring to his tanyard and offered any surplus water to the people of the town.[60] By the time of the Revolution, however, there existed in America no major system for pumping water from a rural reservoir and conveying it to an urban center.

At the close of the century, Americans were to advance beyond the simple schemes of the colonial era and create a system of water supply of unprecedented sophistication. For in 1799 the Philadelphia corporation hired Benjamin Latrobe to plan and supervise the construction of a waterworks along the Schuykill River, to alleviate the serious shortage of water for drinking and firefighting.[61] Steam engines would pump water from the Schuykill into a reservoir and a network of pipes would then carry one million gallons of water into the city each day. Despite some doubts concerning the feasibility of Latrobe's "ridiculous project," the works were supplying the city as early as 1801, and Philadelphians soon enjoyed the benefits of this progressive scheme.[62]

Among those seeking to follow the innovative lead of Philadelphia's corporation were the municipal leaders of New York City. Throughout the late eighteenth and early nineteenth centuries, New York City's aldermen debated the question of constructing a waterworks, returning to the subject periodically for fifty years.[63] In 1799 the committee which investigated the sources of pestilence cited the "healthful effects of a plentiful supply of fresh water" and recommended "that some plan for its introduction into this city be carried into execution as soon as possible."[64] But the city council failed to successfully implement this proposal, and not until the construction of the Croton Aqueduct in the 1830s did New York enjoy a system of water supply equal to that of Philadelphia.

Other municipalities also sought to emulate Philadelphia's achievement and provide wholesome water for an expanding urban citizenry. As early as 1804 New Haven's corporation began construction of an aqueduct, but a shortage of funds soon brought a premature end to this ambitious project.[65] Six years later the borough government of Wilmington, Delaware, purchased a private water company, and from that date the municipality maintained a system of pipes and cisterns which transported water from spring-fed reservoirs to the city's center.[66] By 1830 other towns such as Lancaster, Pennsylvania, and Nashville, Tennessee, were also investing public funds and energies in building similar waterworks,[67] and by mid-century such works were a standard feature of America's largest municipalities.

During these years, municipal advances in water technology were matched by a growing interest in city beautification. Traditionally aldermen and councillors had been oblivious to the physical appearance of their communities, caring little about the merits or demerits of the urban landscape. But by the close of the eighteenth century the municipal corporation of New York City had transformed the Battery area into a "pleasant promenade excelled by none in the United States," where "gravel walks are neatly laid out . . . [and] the shrubbery are delightfully disposed."[68] The city also converted the former town commons into a public garden known simply as "the Park," and in 1804 the corporation ordered New York's street commissioners to determine "what grounds ought to be retained or procured by the Common Council for . . . pleasure grounds . . . or for ornamenting the City in its future growth and extension."[69] Two years later New York's common council took still another step in its campaign to bring sylvan beauty to the booming metropolis. Responding to a petition from a group of tree-loving citizens, the councillors recommended that all those residing along the city's wider streets place trees "in front of their respective houses and lots, not more than twelve feet apart."[70] Thus the city's bustling byways would become shady avenues pleasing to the discriminating eye.

Philadelphians also actively sought to beautify their city by creating parks and planting trees. William Penn's original plan of Philadelphia, drafted in 1682, had provided for five public squares, and during the following 140 years these areas served as burial grounds, cattle markets, pasturelands, city dumps, and fairgrounds. By the early nineteenth century, however, the city council was anxious to transform the squares into green and shaded oases amid the pavement and brick of the expanding metropolis. In 1817 the city hired an engineer to lay out Washington Square for public use and a gardener to supervise the planting of trees. By the late 1820s the improved square was open to Philadelphians, who might stroll along "a handsome, recreative and interesting promenade amongst fifty varieties of trees . . . , a large proportion of which are from distant parts of the Union." Moreover, the local horticultural society further described the park as "beautifully kept and well illuminated at night with reflecting lamps till ten o'clock, all showing the correct and liberal spirit of our city."[71] Improvement of the other squares followed as Philadelphians continued to demonstrate their correct and liberal spirit with regard to urban beautification.

In Savannah, Georgia, the municipal fathers embarked on a similar program to beautify their city. In 1795 they appropriated two hundred dollars for planting trees along the shoreline of Savannah Bay, and in 1807 the corporation established the office of superintendent of trees to care for the city's foliage. Three years later the corporation expended more than a thousand dollars for planting trees in four of the city's public squares and along two of the main streets. And for the pleasure of strolling ladies and gentlemen, the city laid out a network of walks through the landscaped squares.[72]

To preserve these parks and tree-lined avenues, America's municipal leaders also enacted a series of ordinances which outlawed the destruction of urban greenery. For example, in 1806 the Charleston city council forbade anyone to "willfully break down, destroy, injure, or remove any of the trees, . . . growing . . . on the edge of any foot pavement in the city."[73] The following year Baltimore's lawmakers also enacted a measure punishing persons who "hurt or destroy any tree or trees which are . . . planted near the kerb or gutter," and Albany's municipal code of 1808 likewise penalized those "injuring any poplar or other tree" planted under the direction of the superintendent of streets.[74] Moreover, in New York City, the common council attempted to preserve the appearance of the Park and Battery by forbidding anyone from playing "ball, quoits, or any other sport" in these landscaped gardens.[75] Such legislation was only the first step in a long-term effort to fulfill the ideal of the city beautiful. Not until the mid-nineteenth century, however, would this trend finally reach culmination with the opening of such giant parklands as Central Park in New York City, Fairmont Park in Philadelphia, and Druid Hill Park in Baltimore.

While city leaders were exploring the new fields of health, water, and urban beautification, they were also making notable advances in the more established areas of municipal endeavor. For example, such municipalities as New York City and Philadelphia extended their efforts at street construction during this period, hiring salaried commissioners to supervise paving and repair work.[76] Moreover, by 1815 Philadelphia's common council was considering the introduction of gas lamps, and two years later the aldermen of New York City also debated whether to install this new type of streetlight.[77] Even in the western city of Pittsburgh the municipal fathers were attempting to provide modern amenities, and in 1802 they ordered construction of sidewalks paved with "Brick, Stone, or Gravel, bounded by Gutters, and defended Outside by Street Posts."[78] Elsewhere urban officials were purchasing the most advanced forms of fire-fighting equipment, appropriating money for drainage projects, and enlisting an ever increasing number of night watchmen. From Maine to Georgia America's cities were growing rapidly in population, while the level of technology in the Western world was rising at an unprecedented rate. But throughout this period of flux and innovation the municipal corporation adjusted successfully to the varying currents of change.

To pay for these new and changing programs, municipal authorities drew on fresh sources of revenue. Whereas none of the colonial city charters had mentioned the power to levy taxes, virtually all the charters granted after the Revolution bestowed this authority.[79] For example, Charleston's charter of 1783 vested the city councilmen "with full power and authority to make such assessments... as shall appear to them expedient."[80] The Hartford charter of 1784 likewise specified that "all charges and expenses that shall accrue ... shall be borne and defrayed by taxes on the polls of the inhabitants of said city, and the ratable estate contained within said limits."[81] And Baltimore's charter of 1796 granted the corporation "full power and authority ... to lay and collect taxes, not exceeding two dollars in the hundred pounds in any one year."[82]

Some corporations, however, retained their colonial charters, and consequently they could not levy poll or property taxes without specific authorization from the state legislature. For example, New York City continued to operate under its charter of 1730, and each year it sought and received the legislature's permission to exact taxes from the city's residents and property holders. Despite the inconvenience of obtaining this annual authorization, the city grew increasingly dependent on tax revenues. Thus as early as 1790 income derived from taxation accounted for two-thirds of the municipal revenue, while such traditional mainstays as license fees and rents on corporation-owned docks, ferries, and market

TABLE 4   Content Distribution of
City Ordinances, 1803–8

Content	New York City 1805	Albany 1808	Philadelphia 1805	Charleston 1807	New London 1805	New Haven 1803
Trade	32.8%	26.4%	38.5%	28.7%	16.1%	15.7%
Annoyance	16.6%	9.1%	6.6%	5.6%	15.6%	22.4%
Public Safety and Order	25.0%	29.2%	4.7%[a]	15.7%	39.6%	42.2%
Public Works	6.1%	10.0%	23.5%	5.7%	1.8%	1.8%
Administration	4.9%	11.8%	23.7%	24.9%	21.9%	12.7%
Other	15.1%	13.5%	2.9%	19.4%	4.9%	5.2%

NOTE: *Laws of Albany: Ordinances Enacted by the Mayor and Common Council of New-York City* (New York, 1805); *Ordinances and Laws Relating to Philadelphia* (Philadelphia, 1805); Alexander Edwards, ed., *Ordinances of the City Council of Charleston . . . Passed Since the Incorporation of the City* (Charleston, 1807); *Bye Laws of the City of New Haven in Connecticut* (New Haven, 1803); *New London, Conn. By-Laws* (New London, 1805).

[a]This figure is unusually low, probably because Philadelphia's Board of Health rather than Philadelphia's municipal corporation enacted all ordinances concerning health. Consequently virtually no health measures appear in the Philadelphia code of 1805.

stalls totaled only one-third.[83] By the beginning of the nineteenth century commercial rents and fees had definitely assumed a secondary position in municipal ledgers as cities throughout the nation increasingly turned to property and poll taxes for their much-needed revenues.

A numerical analysis of municipal ordinances from the early nineteenth century reveals the magnitude of these changes in legislation and taxation. For as priorities shifted, the content of municipal ordinance books likewise varied, reflecting new attitudes toward trade regulation as well as a growing concern for questions of health, water, urban beautification, and property taxation. Thus a measurement of content distribution for the years 1803–8 reveals no overwhelming concentration of legislative effort in the field of trade and commerce but rather a dispersion of activity over a wide range of subject areas.

By comparing the figures for 1803–8 with those for 1705–24, this shift in the focus of municipal business becomes increasingly apparent (see tables 1 and 4). Whereas in 1710–24 60 percent of Albany's ordinances dealt with trade, by 1808 this figure had dropped to only 26 percent. Likewise, in New York City the figures for trade plummeted from 54 percent in 1707 to approximately 33 percent in 1805. Meanwhile the amount of legislation which focused on safety and order increased markedly during this century, and new laws dealing with taxation and financing swelled percentages in the column headed "administration." No longer was Albany's corporation dedicated primarily to promoting and regulating the Indian trade, or did New York City's corporation in 1805 focus its attention preeminently on issues of vocational opportunity or equitable dealing. Rather, in these cities and in New Haven, Philadelphia, and Charleston as well, the municipal corporation had diversified its activities in a successful attempt to confront the varied problems of urban life.

3   Epilogue

8 The Municipal Revolution Realized

Throughout the last three-quarters of the nineteenth century, the municipal corporation continued to move still further from the ancient model of the commercial community. In every state, political reformers sought to eradicate the last vestiges of autocratic rule, dedicating themselves to the realization of universal manhood suffrage and a three-branch distribution of government power. At the same time, urban leaders urged the development of parks, boulevards, water pipelines, and sewage systems while also advocating the elimination of various forms of commercial regulation. Expansion, change, and adaptation were the watchwords of the age. For during the period 1725 to 1825 Americans had formulated a new pattern of urban rule, and the remaining years of the nineteenth century were dedicated to carrying out this scheme.

Thus reformers continued to tinker with the structure of municipal government in an effort to realize the ideal urban polity. Charter revisions sought to better distribute the powers of government by enhancing the responsibilities of the mayor, reducing the authority of the aldermen, creating new departments and destroying old ones, and sorting out the tangled lines of authority within the municipal structure. Mayors and legislators continued to argue about the exact nature of the state-local relationship, attempting to refine the basic rule of legislative ascendancy formulated in the struggles of the late eighteenth and early nineteenth centuries. In the years following 1825, structural reform became a national fetish as the spirit of experimintation, revision, and change continued to motivate America's city leaders.

Amid this atmosphere of tinkering, arguing, and juggling, the basic principles of the municipal revolution continued to serve as foundation stones for the structure of urban rule. Municipal leaders of the nineteenth and twentieth centuries remained dedicated to the notion of representative government based on a broad suffrage and expressed no desire to return to the autocratic structure of the closed corporation. Likewise, the principle of state ascendancy remained an essential feature of American law even after home-rule charters had introduced some measure of municipal autonomy. In other words, the changes of the eighteenth and early nineteenth centuries had a long-ranging effect, not lessened by the revisions and reforms of later years.

In the field of economic regulation, the doctrines and views developed during the period 1725 to 1825 also continued to influence the course of municipal history. For example, in 1843 New York City's common council finally repealed the measure requiring all beef, pork, lamb, and fish to be sold in the municipality's market houses.[1] And in Chicago a similar piece of legislation disappeared from the city ordinance books in the 1850s. Butchers had long violated such measures, and now the municipal fathers chose to achieve an accord between law and reality. Gradually the public market was declining in influence, and a new retail pattern was developing, with the individual shop and shopkeeper assuming a place of prime importance. Thus market ordinances joined bread price schedules, freeman's privileges, and trade monopolies on the list of repealed or discarded municipal measures.

As the commercial functions of the municipality continued to decline, so the various noneconomic duties of city government continued to expand. Municipally financed art museums, libraries, zoos, public baths, and park systems all appeared during the latter part of the nineteenth century. By the 1890s New York City spent $40,000 a year for concerts in the public parks, and Philadelphia appropriated $15,000 annually for this purpose.[2] Urban reformers strongly advocated greater municipal expenditures for fountains, statues, monuments, and decorative murals in an effort to remold Chicago and Kansas City into latter-day versions of classical Athens and Renaissance Florence.[3] Likewise, municipal efforts at protecting public health and safety grew increasingly sophisticated with the advent of the professional police force and the construction of large-scale municipal hospitals and clinics. In the 1890s as in the 1790s America's cities confronted a growing concern for broader services and unprecedented programs, and the flexible, general-purpose municipal corporation attempted to satisfy these new demands and heightened expectations.

The trends, doctrines, and ideas formulated during the eighteenth and early nineteenth centuries, then, continued to influence the development of the American municipality. The principles of broad-based representative rule, adversary politics, and ascendant state power guided the course of city government throughout future decades. And the ideal of a diffuse-purpose municipality resulted in an ever expanding range of civic functions. This transformation in the nature of municipal business, however, was not necessarily a consequence of changing political structure or practice. The closed corporation of Liverpool was experimenting with new responsibilites and duties more than half a century before the English structural reforms of the 1830s, and the self-elected aldermen of Norfolk, Virginia, were purchasing fire equipment and streetlamps years before the political upheaval of the American Revolution. Both structural and functional changes were a product of fresh social and intellectual currents, but neither was predicated upon the other. Moreover, during the following decades this pattern persisted. The nature of municipal business continued to adapt to the new demands of a new age just as the political life of the municipality adjusted to changing ideology. During the period 1725 to 1825 Americans adapted to new ideas and fresh perceptions, firmly establishing the broad principles underlying modern urban rule in the nineteenth and twentieth centuries.

The acceptance of these basic principles had been a slow and gradual process, which had lasted for many decades. America's first settlers had imported a pattern of urban government from the Old World and planted it firmly in England's colonies. An emerging concern for political and economic liberty as well as material progress had motivated men to deviate from this inherited scheme first in New England and then elsewhere in America. By the eighteenth century the focus of Western thought was on liberating man and harnessing nature. Natural phenomena like fire and disease no longer seemed beyond control. Moreover, man was now able to exploit steam power and use it to pump water into burgeoning urban centers. Nature was no longer an insuperable foe, but an element which could be tamed and manicured in urban parks and public squares. And as the conception of man and nature changed, a new model of urban government developed—a model better suited to the desires and beliefs of the nineteenth century. It was this model of broad representative rule and expansive municipal purpose that would determine the development of the American city.

Notes

Chapter 1

1. The two exceptions are the small boroughs of Bossiney and Havering-atte-Bower. At Carmalthen, Dover, and Sandwich, freeholding was one of several means for acquiring the status of freeman. Sidney and Beatrice Webb, *English Local Government from the Revolution to the Municipal Corporations Act: The Manor and the Borough* (London, 1908), 2:294.

2. The qualifications for admission to freeman status varied somewhat among the English boroughs. In Aldeburgh, Coventry, and Daventry the corporation restricted admission solely to those having served an apprenticeship. Ibid. 1:296. In Berwick-upon-Tweed, on the other hand, freeman status could not be purchased but could be inherited. Ibid. 2:510.

3. George Chandler, *Liverpool under James I* (Liverpool, 1960), p.13. Three of Liverpool's mayors during this period were nonresident freemen. Office-holding by nonresident freemen, however, was not permitted in some boroughs. See J. Dennett, ed., *Beverley Borough Records, 1575–1821* (Wakefield, U.K., 1933), p. 39.

4. Angelo Raine, ed., *York Civic Records* (York, 1953), 8:3, 9-10. The trades represented were merchants, mercers, drapers, apothecaries, goldsmiths, dyers, skinners, barbers, fishmongers, tailors, vintners, joiners, glaziers, hosiers, vestment makers, bowers, innkeepers, wax chandlers, weavers, walkers, saddlers, bakers, glovers, ironmongers, masons, butchers, and pewterers.

5. Webb and Webb, *Manor and Borough*, 2:496-97. The jurymen of Norwich's Court of Mayoralty were also apportioned according to occupation. William L. Sachse, ed., *Minutes of the Norwich Court of Mayoralty 1630-1631* (Norwich, 1942), pp. 57-58, 167-68.

6. Webb and Webb, *Manor and Borough*, 2:569-692.

7. Ibid., pp. 529-58.

8. Ibid., pp. 504-29.

9. Ibid., 1:368.

10. W. H. Stevenson, ed., *Records of the Borough of Nottingham* (London, 1889), 3:341.

11. Ibid., 4:424-32.

12. Information collected from William H. Turner, ed., *Selections from the Records of the City of Oxford* (Oxford, 1880).

13. Edward Cheyney, *A History of England From the Defeat of the Armada to the Death of Elizabeth* (New York, 1948), pp. 7, 9.

14. Stevenson, *Records of Nottingham*, 4:324. All quotations from city

records have been rewritten according to modern English spelling, but the original capitalization has been retained.

15. J. M. Guilding, ed., *Reading Records, Diary of the Corporation* (London, 1895), 2:170, 177, 178, 181, 274-75, 286, 292, 350.

16. Computed from the Liverpool Town Book as reprinted in Chandler, *Liverpool under James I*, pp. 105-298.

17. Edgar I. Fripp, ed., *Minutes and Accounts of the Corporation of Stratford-upon-Avon and Other Records, 1553–1620* (Oxford, 1921), 1:46. See similar measures recorded in Mary Bateson, ed., *Records of the Borough of Leicester* (Cambridge, 1905), 3:ii; and J. W. F. Hill, *Tudor and Stuart Lincoln* (Cambridge, 1956), p. 217.

18. J. Charles Cox, *The Records of the Borough of Northampton* (London, 1898), 2:296.

19. Ibid., p. 303.

20. Turner, *Records of Oxford*, pp. 120-22.

21. Dennett, *Beverley Records*, p. 82; and Fripp, *Minutes of Stratford*, 1:57.

22. Raine, *York Records*, 8:62.

23. Guilding, *Reading Records*, 2:108.

24. For examples of municipal determination of bread and beer prices, see Bateson, *Records of Leicester*, 3:28, 100, 109; Fripp, *Minutes of Stratford*, 1:56, 60, 73, 84-85; A. E. Gibbs, ed., *The Corporation Records of St. Albans* (Saint Albans, U.K., 1890), pp. 54, 95; Cox, *Records of Northampton*, 2:279; *Report on the Records of the City of Exeter* (London, 1916), pp. 316, 395; and Sachse, *Minutes of Norwich Court*, pp. 60, 63, 102.

25. Bateson, *Records of Leicester*, 3:88, 100; Turner, *Records of Oxford*, p. 212; Fripp, *Minutes of Stratford*, 1:47; Dennett, *Beverley Records*, pp. 5, 6, 33; and William Herbert, *The History of the Twelve Great Livery Companies of London* (London, 1834), 1:130. Also see Hill, *Tudor and Stuart Lincoln*, p. 217.

26. Raine, *York Records*, 7:30; 8:62-63.

27. Dennett, *Beverley Records*, p. 84; Herbert, *Livery Companies*, 1:131.

28. Chandler, *Liverpool under James I*, pp. 144, 165, 179, 225; P. Rutledge, ed., "Great Yarmouth Assembly Minutes 1538–1545," *Norfolk Record Society* 39 (1970): 45.

29. Computed from the Liverpool Town Book as reprinted in Chandler, *Liverpool under James I*, pp. 105-298.

30. Cox, *Records of Northampton*, 2:278.

31. Raine, *York Records*, 8:133.

32. Dennet, *Beverley Records*, pp. 81, 83.

33. Raine, *York Records*, 7:54; 8:61.

34. From Corporation Minutes as reprinted in T. Pape, *Newcastle-under-Lyme in Tudor and Early Stuart Times* (Manchester, 1938), p. 221; Bateson, *Records of Leicester*, 3:103.

35. Bateson, *Records of Leicester*, 3:103, 478-87.

36. Gibbs, *Records of St. Albans*, vol. 2.

37. Pape, *Newcastle-under-Lyme*, pp. 57-58; J. R. Boyle, ed., *Charters and Letters Patent Granted to Kingston upon Hull* (Hull, 1905), p. 173; Rutledge, "Great Yarmouth Minutes," p. 20.

38. *Records of Exeter*, pp. 70-71.

39. Raine, *York Records*, 7:1, 3, 4, 8.

40. Guilding, *Reading Records*, 2:284, 360, 370.

41. Ibid., p. 188.

42. Computed from Raine, *York Records*, vols. 7 and 8.

43. Dennett, *Beverley Records*, pp. 36-50, 51-86. A similar survey of what survives of the Oxford records for 1533–83 reveals a total of 144 citations relative to the regulation and promotion of trade (including admissions to the commerce of the borough) as compared with 18 entries dealing with street maintenance and repair, fire and crime prevention, health, and poor relief. Turner, *Oxford Records*.

44. Computed from the Liverpool Town Book as reprinted in Chandler, *Liverpool under James I*, pp. 110-72. In fourth place was gambling, with only 18 prosecutions.

45. Computed from Sachse, *Minutes of Norwich Court*.

46. Chandler, *Liverpool under James I*, pp. 41-83.

47. Guilding, *Reading Records*, 2:240, 252, 473; Rutledge, "Great Yarmouth Minutes," pp. 51, 53-54, 55.

48. Cox, *Records of Northampton*, 2:158; Chandler, *Liverpool under James I*, p. 57.

49. W. T. Baker, ed., *Records of the Borough of Nottingham* (London, 1900), 5:181; L. J. Ashford, *The History of the Borough of High Wycombe from Its Origins to 1880* (London, 1960), pp. 92, 125.

50. Chandler, *Liverpool under James I*, p. 57; William B. Willcox, *Gloucestershire: A Study in Local Government, 1590–1640* (New Haven, Conn., 1940), pp. 148-49.

51. Tom Atkinson, *Elizabethan Winchester* (London, 1963), p. 128.

52. Cox, *Records of Northampton*, 2:153-65.

53. Bateson, *Records of Leicester*, 3:237, 355-56, 426, 444.

54. *Seasonable Reflections on Dissolving Corporation, In the Late Two Reigns, by Surrendering of, and Giving Judgment Against Charters* . . . (London, 1689), p. 25.

Chapter 2

1. Edward P. Allinson and Boies Penrose, *Philadelphia, 1681–1887* (Baltimore, 1887), p. xlvi; M. Carey and J. Bioren, eds., *Laws of the Commonwealth of Pennsylvania, 1700–1802* (Philadelphia, 1803), vol. 6, Appendix, p. 21.

2. Carey and Bioren, *Laws of Pennsylvania*, vol. 6, Appendix, p. 23; *The Charter of the City of New Brunswick of December 30, 1730 and Early Ordinances of the City* (New Brunswick, 1913), p. 7.

3. Elihu S. Riley, *The Ancient City: A History of Annapolis, in Maryland* (Annapolis, 1887), p. 87.

4. Austin Scott, "The Early Cities of New Jersey," *Proceedings of the New Jersey Historical Society*, 2nd ser., 9 (1886–87): 153.

5. These municipalities are listed as follows, with their dates of incorporation: New York City, 1653, 1665 (first English charter), 1686, 1731; Albany, 1686; Philadelphia, 1691, 1701; Chester, Pennsylvania, 1701; Annapolis, 1708; Perth Amboy, 1718; Bristol, Pennsylvania, 1720; Williamsburg, 1722; New

Brunswick, New Jersey, 1730; Burlington, New Jersey, 1733; Norfolk, 1736; Wilmington, Delaware, 1739; Elizabeth, New Jersey, 1740; and Lancaster, Pennsylvania, 1742. Other towns such as Saint Marys, Maryland, Germantown, Pennsylvania, and Westchester, New York, received charters before 1750, but borough government did not survive in these communities. Notably absent from the list is the largest American urban center of 1700, Boston, Massachusetts. For a description of Boston's form of government see chapter 3.

6. Computed from *Several Laws, Orders & Ordinances Established by the Mayor, Recorder, Aldermen and Assistants of the City of New-York, Conven'd in Common-Council, for the Good Rule and Government of the Inhabitants of the Said City* (New York, 1707).

7. Computed from the City Records as contained in Joel Munsell, ed., *The Annals of Albany* (Albany, 1854–59).

8. Computed from *Minutes of the Common Council of the City of Philadelphia, 1704 to 1776* (Philadelphia, 1847). I have classified the ordinances according to the apparent motive for their enactment. In the trade category are all ordinances enacted to guarantee fair dealing, allocate vocational privileges, and construct or maintain such commercial facilities as docks or markets. The annoyance rubric covers provisions relative to street encroachment, rubbish, posts, or wood in the streets, slaughterhouse odor and filth, and animals running loose. The borough fathers regarded these subjects as an annoyance or inconvenience but not necessarily as a danger to the safety or property of the community. Ordinances dealing with such dangers fall within the category of public safety and order. Among these are measures regulating the night watch, the sale of liquor to hostile Indians, fire prevention, and the behavior of Negroes at night. I have defined public works as including the paving and repair of streets, and legislation relative to water pumps, stockades, and the surveying of the city. On the other hand, the administration column includes ordinances concerning the municipal officers and procedures of a general nature such as the municipal seal or the corporation treasurer. In the "other" category are a variety of provisions dealing with corporation property, Sabbath regulation, and the licensing of liquor retailers. Colonial boroughs enacted such liquor licensing laws primarily for reasons of revenue and the regulation of immoral conduct. Consequently I have placed these within the miscellaneous group.

9. *Charter and Early Ordinances of New Brunswick*, pp. 32, 63–64.

10. Munsell, *Annals of Albany*, 2:79–80; *The Colonial Laws of New York From the Year 1664 to the Revolution* (Albany, 1894), 2:615–16; Nicholas Murray, *Notes, Historical and Biographical, Concerning Elizabeth-town, Its Eminent Men, Churches and Ministers* (Elizabeth, 1844), p. 35; *Charter and Early Ordinances of New Brunswick*, p. 20.

11. Munsell, *Annals of Albany*, 3:50–51, 51–52; 4:142–43; 6:258; 7:172–73; 8:279, 294, 297.

12. "The Burghers of New Amsterdam and the Freemen of New York, 1675–1866," *Collections of the New-York Historical Society For the Year 1885* 18:50.

13. Samuel McKee, Jr., *Labor in Colonial New York, 1664–1776* (New York, 1935), p. 30.

14. *Charter and Early Ordinances of New Brunswick*, p. 44.

15. *Minutes of the Council of Philadelphia*, pp. 34, 73.

16. Ibid., pp. 118-35.

17. *Freeman's Journal; or North American Intelligencer*, 8 Oct. 1781; *Pennsylvania Packet, and Daily Advertiser*, 30 Aug. 1786.

18. *Minutes of the Common Council of the City of New York, 1675–1776* (New York, 1905), 2:264.

19. Ibid., p. 355. For another example see ibid., p. 278.

20. Munsell, *Annals of Albany*, 7:171.

21. *Minutes of the Council of New York, 1675–1776*, 1:135; Berthold Fernow, ed., *The Records of New Amsterdam From 1653 to 1674 Anno Domini* (New York, 1897), 5:312.

22. *Minutes of the Council of New York, 1675–1776*, 1:21, 22, 24.

23. Ibid., 4:106.

24. "Minutes of the Borough of Lancaster, Pennsylvania," Office of City Clerk, Lancaster, Pennsylvania, 13 Sept. 1742.

25. Munsell, *Annals of Albany*, 2:80-83.

26. Ibid., pp. 95-97.

27. Ibid., 5:159-62.

28. Ibid., 7:236-37, 269. For other cases centering on the violation of Albany's Indian trade ordinances, see ibid., 2:114, 118-19, 129-30, 3:52; 4:182-83; 5:166-67.

29. Allen W. Trelease, *Indian Affairs in Colonial New York: The Seventeenth Century* (Ithaca, N.Y., 1960), p. 223.

30. Munsell, *Annals of Albany*, 8:210-11, 212.

31. Carey and Bioren, *Laws of Pennsylvania*, vol. 6, Appendix, pp. 22, 25.

32. *Minutes of the Council of New York, 1675–1776*, 1:140-41; 2:13, 25; *Charter and Early Ordinances of New Brunswick*, pp. 70-72; "Minutes of Lancaster," 28 Sept. 1744, Ernest Griffith, *History of American City Government: The Colonial Period* (New York, 1938), p. 148; Scott, "Early Cities of New Jersey," p. 169; Munsell, *Annals of Albany*, 2:12; 5:143, 179-80; 6:288; 7:30, 55-56, 57, 176.

33. *Minutes of the Council of Philadelphia*, pp. 147, 164-65; Munsell, *Annals of Albany*, 6:257; *Minutes of the Council of New York, 1675–1776*, 2:72, 131-32; 4:297-98; 6:256-57.

34. Richard B. Morris, *Government and Labor in Early America* (New York, 1946), pp. 161-62; Fernow, *Records of New Amsterdam*, 1:43-44, 47-48; 2:119; 3:378, 381-91; 4:218; 7:206, 215, 219-20, 221. Albany Mayor's Court Minutes, 3 Nov. 1691, as cited in Morris, *Government and Labor*, p. 162; Munsell, *Annals of Albany*, 2:115; *Minutes of the Council of New York, 1675–1776*, 1:254, 256.

35. *Minutes of the Council of New York, 1675-1776*, 1:64-65.

36. Ibid., pp. 147-48.

37. Ibid., p. 393.

38. Ibid., p. 140.

39. Munsell, *Annals of Albany*, 8:259-60.

40. *Charter and Early Ordinances of New Brunswick*, p. 26; David Ridgeley, ed., *Annals of Annapolis, Comprising Sundry Notices of That Old City* (Baltimore, 1841), p. 122.

41. "Minutes of Lancaster," 25 January 1746.

42. Munsell, *Annals of Albany*, 3:12-13.

43. Fernow, *Records of New Amsterdam*, vol. 6; 3:214-15.

44. *Minutes of the Council of New York, 1675-1776*, 4:85, 293.

45. *Minutes of the Council of Philadelphia*, pp. 81, 83, 164, 272.

46. "Minutes of Lancaster," 9 October 1744.

47. Munsell, *Annals of Albany*, 8:170.

48. *Charter and Early Ordinances of New Brunswick*, p. 26; *Minutes of the Council of New York, 1675-1776*, 4:95.

49. *Minutes of the Council of New York, 1675-1776*, 2:454-55.

50. Based on figures in Morris, *Government and Labor*, p. 371, and Paul H. Douglas, *American Apprenticeship and Industrial Education* (New York, 1921), p. 40.

51. *Minutes of the Council of Philadelphia*, p. 147.

52. Based on information in David Valentine, ed., *Manual of the Common Council of New York for 1860* (New York, 1859), pp. 481-520.

53. Computed on the basis of information in Judith Diamondstone, "The Philadelphia Corporation, 1701–1776," Ph.D. diss., University of Pennsylvania, 1969, pp. 256-57.

54. Ibid., pp. 251-52.

55. *Valentine's Manual for 1860*, pp. 481-520.

56. Diamondstone, "Philadelphia Corporation," p. 251.

57. Ibid., p. 251; Judith Diamondstone, "Philadelphia's Municipal Corporation, 1701–1776," *Pennsylvania Magazine of History and Biography* 90 (Apr. 1966): 194.

58. Four members of the Schuyler family served as mayor of Albany during the first forty years of the city's existence. "Notes and Queries," *New York Genealogical and Biographical Record*, 20 (Jan. 1889): 42-43.

59. Henry G. Ashmead, *Historical Sketch of Chester* (Chester, Pa., 1883), p. 74.

60. Based on "New-York Tax Lists 1695–1699", *Collections of the New-York Historical Society for the Year 1911*, vol. 44.

61. Henry Collins Brown, ed., *Valentine's Manual of Old New York, 1925* (New York, 1924), pp. 151-53, 156-57.

62. "New York Tax Lists," *Coll. of N.Y. Hist. Soc.*, 44:228-31.

63. John A. Fairlie, "Municipal Corporations in the Colonies," *Municipal Affairs*, 2 (Sept. 1898): 366; *Colonial Laws of New York*, 2:584; Munsell, *Annals of Albany*, 2:74.

64. Murray, *Notes Concerning Elizabeth-town*, p. 40; Carey and Bioren, *Laws of Pennsylvania*, vol. 6, Appendix, p. 17. The charter of New Brunswick grants a jurisdictional authority similar to that of Elizabeth. *Charter and Early Ordinances of New Brunswick*, p. 17.

65. Riley, *Annapolis*, p. 91; "The Building of Williamsburg," *William and Mary Quarterly Historical Magazine*, 1st ser., 10 (Oct. 1901): 90; *The Ordinances of Norfolk* (Norfolk, 1829), p. 8.

66. Fernow, *Records of New Amsterdam*, 6:73.

67. Ibid., p. 139.

68. Richard B. Morris, ed., *Select Cases of the Mayor's Court of New York City, 1674-1784* (Washington, D.C., 1935), p. 40.

69. "Minutes of Lancaster"; Griffith, *American City Government*, p. 301.

70. Riley, *Annapolis*, p. 90; "Building of Williamsburg," p. 89; "Norfolk Borough Council Orders," Office of City Clerk, Norfolk, Virginia, 20 Dec. 1736.

71. Fairlie, "Municipal Corporations in the Colonies," p. 377; *Minutes of the Council of Philadelphia*, p. 109.

72. "Burghers and Freemen," pp. 47, 50, 51, 451. Computation based on bread prices as fixed by the cities of New York and Albany.

73. Munsell, *Annals of Albany*, 7:173.

74. Computed on basis of figures in "Ledger Number I, Chamberlain's Office, Corporation of the City of New York," *Collections of the New-York Historical Society* 42 (1909): 1–110.

75. Munsell, *Annals of Albany*, 2:65–66. *Colonial Laws of New York*, 2:578.

76. Munsell, *Annals of Albany*, 2:67.

77. George Edwards and Arthur Peterson, *New York as an Eighteenth Century Municipality* (New York, 1917), p. 82.

78. *Colonial Laws of New York*, 2:645–48; 3:158–62.

79. William W. Hening, ed., *The Statutes at Large; Being A Collection of all the Laws of Virginia, From the First Session of the Legislature, in the Year 1619* (Richmond, 1810–23), 5:263–64.

80. Estimate based on figures in "Ledger Number I," pp. 1–110.

81. Carey and Bioren, *Laws of Pennsylvania*, vol. 6, Appendix, p. 18; "Building of Williamsburg," p. 86; *Ordinances of Norfolk*, p. 5.

82. *Charter and Early Ordinances of New Brunswick*, p. 15; Murray, *Notes Concerning Elizabeth-town*, p. 43; Munsell, *Annals of Albany*, 2:74; *Laws of New York*, 2:605; Griffith, *American City Government*, p. 181. Bristol's charter provided for a town meeting similar to those of Chester and Lancaster, but by 1732 the citizenry had abandoned this means of direct participation.

83. Carey and Bioren, *Laws of Pennsylvania*, vol. 6, Appendix, p. 22; Griffith, *American City Government*, pp. 181–82.

84. *Colonial Laws of New York*, 2:605; Murray, *Notes Concerning Elizabeth-town*, p. 43; *Charter and Early Ordinances of New Brunswick*, p. 15; Griffith, *American City Government*, p. 203. This also seems to have been true of Albany. Fairlie, "Municipal Corporations in the Colonies," p. 354.

85. Carey and Bioren, *Laws of Pennsylvania*, vol. 6, Appendix, p. 19; "Building of Williamsburg," p. 85; *Ordinances of Norfolk*, p. 4; Riley, *Annapolis*, p. 88.

86. Riley, *Annapolis*, p. 89; "Building of Williamsburg," p. 88; *Ordinances of Norfolk*, p. 6.

87. Munsell, *Annals of Albany*, 10:93.

88. *Colonial Laws of New York*, 2:605.

89. Carey and Bioren, *Laws of Pennsylvania*, vol. 6, Appendix, pp. 21, 25; Murray, *Notes Concerning Elizabeth-town*, p. 43; *Charter and Early Ordinances of New Brunswick*, p. 15. In New Brunswick officeholding seems to have been open to freeholders whereas the franchise was restricted to freemen.

90. Carey and Bioren, *Laws of Pennsylvania*, vol. 6, Appendix, p. 19; Riley, *Annapolis*, p. 88; "Building of Williamsburg," p. 86; *Ordinances of Norfolk*, p. 5. For examples of enforcement of freehold and freeman restrictions in New

York City, see *Minutes of the Council of New York 1675–1776*, 4:72, 154, 219, 220, 471.

91. *The New York Gazette Revived in the Weekly Post Boy*, 24 April 1749.

92. Ibid., 17 Apr. 1749.

93. *New York Mercury*, 14 Sept. 1765; Edwin F. Hatfield, *History of Elizabeth, New Jersey* (New York, 1868), pp. 403-4.

94. *New York Weekly Journal*, 7 Oct. 1734.

95. Ibid., 6 Oct. 1735.

96. *Philadelphia Gazette*, 7 October 1736; George Edwards, "New York City Politics before the American Revolution," *Political Science Quarterly* 36 (Dec. 1921): 594.

97. Dr. Alexander Hamilton to M. G. H———at Edinburgh, 20 October 1743, "Dr. Alexander Hamilton's Letter Book, 1739–1743." Dulany Papers, Maryland Historical Society; Aubrey C. Land, *The Dulanys of Maryland* (Baltimore, 1955), p. 187.

98. *Colonial Laws of New York*, 2:583; Scott, "Early Cities of New Jersey," pp. 154-55. New Jersey's royal governor appointed both the mayor and legal counsel in Burlington, but not the clerk. Similarly in Elizabeth he appointed only the legal counsel.

99. See Frederic W. Maitland and Mary Bateson, eds., *The Charters of the Borough of Cambridge* (Cambridge, 1901), p. 187, Christopher A. Markham, *The Records of the Borough of Northampton* (London, 1898), 1:147; J. W. F. Hill, *Tudor and Stuart Lincoln* (Cambridge, 1956), p. 189; and Jennifer Levin, *The Charter Controversy in the City of London, 1660–1688, and Its Consequences* (London, 1969), p. 4.

100. In 1746 the New York provincial assembly did attempt to eliminate the charter restrictions on practicing in the mayor's court of New York City without the corporation's consent, but the province never enforced this measure, Morris, *Cases of the Mayor's Court of New York*, p. 53.

101. Griffith, *American City Government*, p. 111.

102. Scott, "Early Cities of New Jersey," p. 155.

103. Riley, *Annapolis*, p. 89.

Chapter 3

1. Nathaniel B. Shurtleff, ed., *Records of the Governor and Company of the Massachusetts Bay in New England* (Boston, 1853–54), 1:87, 161.

2. *The Acts and Resolves, Public and Private, of the Province of the Massachusetts Bay* (Boston, 1869), 1:65.

3. *Boston Town Records* (Boston, 1883), 8:9-17; *Several Rules, Orders, and By-Laws Made and Agreed Upon by the Freeholders and Inhabitants of Boston* (Boston, 1702). In 1696 the Massachusetts General Court did authorize a public market and two annual fairs in Boston, but efforts to implement this authorization met with almost immediate failure. *Massachusetts Acts and Resolves*, 1:66; *Boston Records*, 7:224; Benjamin Colman, *Some Reasons and Arguments Offered to the Good People of Boston and Adjacent Places for the Setting Up Markets in Boston* (Boston, 1719), p. 9.

4. Anne Bush MacLear, "Early New England Towns: A Comparative Study of Their Development," *Studies in History, Economics and Public Law, 29* (1908): 55-80; *Massachusetts Acts and Resolves*, 1:66.

5. *Massachusetts Acts and Resolves*, 1:66. The selectmen did have some judicial authority before 1692. After the passage of the Town Act of that year, however, enforcement rested in the hands of the county justices. Charles J. Hilkey, "Legal Development in Colonial Massachusetts," *Studies in History, Economics and Public Law*, 37 (1910): 29-50. For an abortive attempt to change this situation, see *Massachusetts Acts and Resolves*, 1:217-19.

6. See, for example, Kenneth A. Lockridge, *A New England Town: The First Hundred Years* (New York, 1970), pp. 106-7, 115-16; Samuel Sewall, *The History of Woburn* (Boston, 1868), pp. 242-59.

7. Joseph B. Felt, "Ancient Application of Boston For A City Charter," *New England Historical and Genealogical Register* 11 (July 1857): 206.

8. Albert Matthews, "Remarks on Attempts to Incorporate Boston," *Publications of the Colonial Society of Boston* 10 (1904–6): 352-56.

9. Felt, "Ancient Application," 11:206-10.

10. "Gowen Anderson, Robert Williams, John Frany and others to the General Court, 1648," Massachusetts Archives, as cited in Darrett B. Rutman, *Winthrop's Boston: Portrait of a Puritan Town, 1630-1649* (Chapel Hill, 1965) pp. 249-50.

11. *Boston Records*, 8:55.

12. Felt, "Ancient Application," 11:206.

13. Colman, *Arguments for the Setting Up Markets in Boston*, p. 7.

14. Ibid., p. 6.

15. Worthington Chauncey Ford, ed., "Communication of Two Documents Protesting against the Incorporation of Boston," *Publications of the Colonial Society of Massachusetts* 10 (1904–6): 346-47. The pamphlets reprinted in this communication date from approximately 1714.

16. Ibid., p. 346.

17. Ibid., p. 349.

18. Colman, *Arguments for the Setting Up Markets in Boston*, p. 11.

19. Ford, "Communication of Two Documents," pp. 346, 349.

20. Colman, *Arguments for the Setting Up Markets in Boston*, p. 8.

21. Ford, "Communication of Two Documents," p. 345.

22. Ibid., p. 349.

23. Ibid., pp. 351-52.

24. Ibid., pp. 346-47.

25. *Boston Records*, 12:80-82; *At a Meeting of the Freeholders, and Other Inhabitants of the Town of Boston* . . . (Boston, 1734).

26. *Boston Records*, 12:134-35.

27. For a general account of the market riots and controversy see G. B. Warden, *Boston 1689-1776* (Boston, 1970), pp. 115–23.

28. *Boston Records*, 12:164, 170-71.

29. Ibid., p. 259.

30. *Boston Evening Post*, 12 Sept. 1763.

Chapter 4

1. *Philadelphia Council Minutes*, p. 271.

2. William Maitland, *The History and Survey of London From Its Foundation to the Present Time* (London, 1756), pp. 677-79.

3. William E. H. Lecky, *A History of England in the Eighteenth Century* (New York, 1883), 1:213-14; Derek Jarrett, *Britain 1688-1815* (London, 1965), p. 334; Evarts B. Greene and Virginia D. Harrington, *American Population before the Federal Census of 1790* (New York, 1932), pp. 95, 100, 117, 118.

4. See, for example, the complaints of London's master painters, who were in need of a greater number of journeymen than were available from the body of freemen. Maitland, *History and Survey of London*, p. 677.

5. K. B. Smellie, *Great Britain since 1688: A Modern History* (Ann Arbor, 1962), p. 130.

6. Adam Smith, *An Inquiry into the Nature and Causes of the Wealth of Nations*, 2d ed. (London, 1778), 1:161.

7. *Critical Observations on the Buildings and Improvements of London* (London, 1771), p. 17, as quoted in Sidney and Beatrice Webb, *Statutory Authorities for Special Purposes* (London, 1922), p. 242.

8. Munsell, ed., *Annals of Albany*, 8:294, 297; *New York Gazette*, 17 Mar. 1755.

9. Beverly McAnear, "The Place of the Freeman in Old New York," *New York History* 21 (Oct. 1940): 423.

10. Webb and Webb, *Manor and Borough*, 1:400.

11. A. Temple Patterson, *A History of Southampton 1700-1914* (Southampton, 1966), 1:36; G. A. Chinnery, ed., *Records of the Borough of Leicester* (Leicester, 1965), 5:189. For the decline of the freeman's monopoly in Lincoln see Sir Francis Hill, *Georgian Lincoln* (Cambridge, 1966), p. 244.

12. Joel Munsell, ed., *Collections on the History of Albany* (Albany, 1867), 2:292.

13. Munsell, *Annals of Albany*, 8:286-90; Jonathan Pearson et al., *A History of the Schenectady Patent in Dutch and English Times* (Albany, 1883), p. 418.

14. Pearson, *Schenectady Patent*, p. 418.

15. Ibid., p. 419.

16. *Minutes of the Council of New York*, 4:97; McKee, *Labor in New York*, p. 72.

17. Carl Bridenbaugh, *The Colonial Craftsmen* (New York, 1950), p. 144.

18. "Norfolk Council Orders," 28 June 1754.

19. *Minutes of the Council of New York*, 6:337-42.

20. Thomas DeVoe, *The Market Book: A History of the Public Markets of the City of New York* (New York, 1862), pp. 148-49.

21. *New York Gazette*, 12 Sept. 1763; DeVoe, *Market Book*, pp. 145-46.

22. *New York Gazette*, 12 Sept. 1763; DeVoe, *Market Book*, p. 146.

23. *New York Gazette*, 19 Sept. 1763; DeVoe, *Market Book*, p. 147.

24. Content analysis based on ordinances contained in the following: "Minutes of the Borough of Lancaster," *Laws and Ordinances of the Mayor, Recorder, Aldermen, and Commonalty, of the City of Albany* (Albany, 1773); *Laws, Statutes, Ordinances and Constitutions, Ordained, Made, and Estab-*

lished by the Mayor, Aldermen and Commonalty of the City of New-York (New York, 1774).

25. *Minutes of the Council of New York*, 4:55, 56.

26. Ibid., p. 367.

27. DeVoe, *Market Book*, p. 259.

28. Lowell Limpus, *History of the New York Fire Department* (New York, 1940), pp. 57-59.

29. Codman Hislop, *Albany: Dutch, English, and American* (Albany, 1936),p. 142.

30. J. Thomas Scharf and Thompson Westcott, *History of Philadelphia, 1609-1884* (Philadelphia, 1884), 1:192-93.

31. *The Bye-Laws of the City of Annapolis in Maryland* (Annapolis, 1769), pp. 33-35; John P. Wall, *The Chronicles of New Brunswick, New Jersey, 1667-1931* (New Brunswick, 1931), p. 54; "Norfolk Council Orders," 11 Sept. 1761.

32. For the reaction of one Tudor-Stuart corporation to the emergency of epidemic, see Cox, *Records of Northampton*, 2:233-40. Also for a general overview of the new currents in health care see chapter 16, "The Eighteenth Century, an Era of Hygiene," in S. G. Blaxland Stubbs and E. W. Bligh, *Sixty Centuries of Health and Physick* (London, 1931).

33. Hening, *Virginia Statutes*, 8:21-23.

34. *Bye-Laws of Annapolis*, pp. 32-33; *Maryland Gazette*, 14 Mar. 1765.

35. *Ordinances of New-York* (1774), pp. 30-32; *Ordinances of Albany*, pp. 59-62.

36. Alice M. Keys, *Cadwallader Colden: A Representative Eighteenth Century Official* (New York, 1906), pp. 24-25; *New-York Weekly Post Boy*, 26 Dec. 1743-9 Jan. 1744. Reprinted in the *Pennsylvania Gazette*, 11 Jan.-2 Feb. 1744.

37. *Laws, Statutes, Ordinances, and Constitutions, Ordained, Made and Established, By the Mayor, Recorder, Aldermen, and Assistants, of the City of New-York* (New York, 1749), p. 28.

38. James Grant Wilson, ed., *The Memorial History of the City of New-York*, (New York, 1892), 1:496.

39. *Colonial Laws of New York*, 4:573-76; Wilson, *History of New York City*, 2:463.

40. "Norfolk Council Orders," 30 Dec. 1765; Hening, *Virginia Statutes*, 7:654-55; Joel Munsell, ed., *Collections on Albany* (Albany, 1864), 1:226.

41. Hening, *Virginia Stautes*, 7:654-55; 8:21-23.

42. *Colonial Laws of New York*, 3:942-47; 4:573-76; 5:611-12.

43. G. A. Chinnery, ed., *Records of the Borough of Leicester* (Leicester, 1965), 5:154, 155-56.

44. Hill, *Georgian Lincoln*, p. 58; Frederick H. Spencer, *Municipal Origins* (London, 1911), p. 163. For street lighting in Nottingham see *Records of the Borough of Nottingham* (Nottingham, 1947), 7:22, 23, 24.

45. Webb and Webb, *Manor and Borough*, 2:483-84.

46. *Philadelphia Council Minutes*, p. 696.

47. Edward P. Allinson and Boes Penrose, eds., "The Early Government of Philadelphia, and the Blue Anchor Tavern Landing," *Pennsylvania Magazine*

of History and Biography 10 (1886); 61-77; *Philadelphia Council Minutes,* pp. 622-25.

48. Webb and Webb, *Manor and Borough,* 2:441-42.

49. Diamondstone, "Philadelphia Corporation," pp. 267, 270.

50. Based on information in Diamondstone, "Philadelphia Corporation," pp. 278, 282.

51. Sixteen percent of the active members ranked within the uppermost 1 percent in terms of wealth. Computed on the basis of the list of members attending meetings in 1773 and the tax assessments for these individuals as recorded in William Henry Egle, ed., *Pennsylvania Archives, Third Series* (Harrisburg, 1897), 14:223-303.

52. Carey and Bioren, *Laws of Pennsylvania,* 1:312, 381; Allinson and Penrose, *Philadelphia, 1681-1887,* pp. 31-33, 36.

53. Webb and Webb, *Statutory Authorities,* p. 244.

54. Silvanus Jackson Quinn, *The History of the City of Fredericksburg, Virginia* (Richmond, 1908), pp. 38-42; Mary G. Powell, *The History of Old Alexandria, Virginia* (Richmond, 1928), pp. 28-31; Hening, *Laws of Virginia,* 6:268-70; *First Records of Baltimore Town and Jones Town, 1729-1797* (Baltimore, 1905); Walter Clark, ed., *The State Records of North Carolina* (Goldsboro, N. C., 1904), 23:136-41, 772-73.

55. Clark, *Records of North Carolina,* 23:146-49, 304-8. In 1763 Wilmington received a royal charter and thus became a municipal corporation.

56. *Minutes of the Council of New York,* 7:252.

57. Ibid., p. 348.

58. "Minutes of the Borough of Lancaster," 18 Feb. 1772.

59. Griffith, *American City Government,* p. 198.

60. *Valentine's Manual of 1860,* pp. 481-520, 523-24, 525-26. The same trend appears for appointed officials in Albany. See "Notes and Queries," *New York Genealogical and Biographical Record* 20 (Jan. 1889): 42-43; Munsell, *Annals of Albany,* 5:101-2. The relatively short terms in office during the late seventeenth and early eighteenth centuries may be due to the Leislerian–Anti-Leislerian factional rivalry of the period. This factional rivalry created considerable instability in New York politics for two decades.

61. Wall, *Chronicles of New Brunswick,* pp. 28-30, William H. Benedict, *New Brunswick in History* (New Brunswick, 1925), pp. 30-31, 36-37.

62. "Minutes of the Borough of Lancaster"; Franklin Ellis and Samuel Evans, *History of Lancaster County, Pennsylvania* (Philadelphia, 1883), p. 373.

63. J. Thomas Scharf, *History of Delaware, 1609-1888* (Philadelphia, 1888), 2:637-39.

64. Computed on basis of information in *Valentine's Manual for 1860,* pp. 481-520; Munsell, *Annals of Albany,* vol. 10, and Munsell, *Collections on the History of Albany,* vols. 1, 2. In contrast, the average length of service on New York City's council during a period of party rivalry such as 1800–1850 was only three years.

65. Computed on the basis of tax assessments recorded in Egle, *Pennsylvania Archives, Third Series,* 17:454-65. All of the Lancaster councilmen ranked above the median for the community in terms of wealth, five of the nine ranked within top 10 percent, and three were among the uppermost 5 percent. Five of

the nine were shopkeepers, one was an innkeeper, one was a barber, and another was a dyer.

66. Milton Klein, ed., *The Independent Reflector; or, Weekly Essays on Sundry Important Subjects* (Cambridge, Mass., 1963), pp. 118-27, 381.

67. William Goddard, *To My Fellow Citizens, Friends to Liberty, and Enemies to Despotism* (Philadelphia, 1773).

68. *To the Freemen, Citizens of Philadelphia*, no. 1 (Philadelphia, 1773); *To the Freemen, Citizens of Philadelphia*, no. 2 (Philadelphia, 1773).

69. William Goddard, *Andrew Marvell's Second Address to the Inhabitants of Philadelphia* (Philadelphia, 1773), p. 12.

70. Goddard, *To My Fellow Citizens.*

71. *To the Freemen, Citizens of Philadelphia*, no. 1

72. Ibid.

Chapter 5

1. The cities receiving charters during this period were: Alexandria, Va., 1779; Winchester, Va., 1779; Fredericksburg, Va., 1781; Richmond, Va., 1782; Charleston, S.C., 1783; Reading, Pa., 1783; Carlisle, Pa., 1783; Petersburg, Va., 1784; Perth Amboy, N.J., 1784; Burlington, N.J., 1784; New Brunswick, N.J., 1784; Norwich, Conn., 1784; New London, Conn., 1784; Middletown, Conn., 1784; Hartford, Conn., 1784; New Haven, Conn., 1784; Newport, R.I., 1784; Hudson, N.Y., 1785; York, Va., 1786; York, Pa., 1787; Savannah, Ga., 1789; Georgetown, Md., 1789; Philadelphia, Pa., 1789; Elizabeth, N.J., 1789; and Easton, Pa., 1789. The state of Georgia also granted a charter to Augusta in 1789, but this seems to have never taken effect. In 1795 the inhabitants of Augusta formally surrendered the document of incorporation. Salem Dutcher and Charles C. Jones, *Memorial History of Augusta, Georgia* (Syracuse, 1890), pp. 158-59.

2. Paul L. Ford, ed., *The Writings of Thomas Jefferson* (New York, 1892-99), pp. 357-61.

3. William Kilty, ed., *The Laws of Maryland* (Annapolis, 1800), vol. 2 (1789), chap. 23, (1797), chap. 56.

4. See a copy of the proposed charter as printed in the *Pennsylvania Gazette*, 4 June 1783.

5. *Pennsylvania Packet; or, General Advertiser*, 2 Sept. 1783.

6. For the charter of 1789 see James T. Mitchell and Henry Flanders, comps., *The Statutes at Large of Pennsylvania from 1682 to 1801* (Harrisburg, Pa., 1911), 13:195-214. Although only Georgetown's charter granted life tenure to councilmen, the charters of Connecticut's cities did grant mayors virtual life tenure. Mayors in Connecticut served until removed by the state legislature, and since the legislature did not intervene mayors often occupied office until they died. The mayors, however, were primarily ceremonial and judicial officers with only minor legislative functions.

7. The one exception was the charter of Elizabeth, New Jersey, granted in 1789. See *Statutes of New Jersey* (Trenton, 1804), pp. 95-96. Though the charters of Connecticut's five cities bestowed no such power on the aldermen, a later act of the legislature did grant very limited authority to admit persons to

an enfranchised status. Under the terms of this act, aldermen could offer such status to any person "living without the limits of said cities." But Connecticut's municipal leaders did not exercise any authority to define the resident electorate of their cities. *The Public Statute Laws of the State of Connecticut* (Hartford, 1808), 1:185. The term "freeman" was also occasionally used in post-Revolutionary charters to denote a man who met the property and residency qualifications for voting. In these cases, however, freeman status bore no relation to commerce and was not granted at the discretion of the city aldermen.

8. David J. McCord and Thomas Cooper, eds., *The Statutes at Large of South Carolina* (Columbia, S.C., 1836–41), 7:97-101; Hening, *Virginia Statutes*, 11:45-50; Mitchell and Flanders, *Statutes of Pennsylvania*, 13:195-214; *Statutes of New Jersey*, pp. 56-63.

9. *Statutes of New Jersey*, pp. 64-74.

10. Carey and Bioren, *Laws of Pennsylvania*, 2:333-52.

11. Hening, *Virginia Statutes*, 10:172-76, 439-43.

12. *Massachusetts Centinel*, 9, 26, 30 Nov. 1785; *American Herald*, 10 May 1784, 31 Oct., 7 Nov. 1785.

13. *Pennsylvania Packet, and Daily Advertiser*, 17 Nov., 30 Dec. 1785; 25, 26 Sept. 1786; 3 Feb. 1789; *Independent Gazetteer; or, Chronicle of Freedom*, 12 Nov. 1785; 6, 28 June 1787; *Federal Gazette, and Philadelphia Evening Post*, 3 Oct. 1788, 31 Jan. 1789.

14. *Massachusetts Centinel: and Republican Journal*, 15 May 1784, 19 Nov. 1785.

15. *Pennsylvania Packet, and Daily Advertiser*, 30 Aug., 25, 26, 27 Sept. 1786.

16. *Maryland Journal and Baltimore Advertiser*, 14 Feb., 12 Sept. 1794.

17. *Newport Mercury*, 5 Mar. 1787.

18. *Maryland Journal and Baltimore Advertiser*, 3 Mar. 1794.

19. *Pennsylvania Packet, and Daily Advertiser*, 25 Sept. 1786.

20. Alfred B. Street, ed., *The Council of Revision of the State of New York* (Albany, 1859), p. 275.

21. *Daily Advertiser*, 10 Apr. 1792.

22. *Newport Mercury*, 2 Oct. 1786.

23. *Massachusetts Centinel*, 26 May 1784.

24. *Boston Gazette and Country Journal*, 7 Nov. 1785.

25. *Massachusetts Centinel*, 30 Nov. 1785.

26. Ibid., 26 Oct. 1785.

27. Ibid., 26 Oct. 1785.

28. Ibid., 26 Oct. 1785. For similar sentiments see also Ibid., 29 Oct., 9 Nov., 19 Nov., 30 Nov. 1785.

29. *Newport Mercury*, 2 Oct. 1786.

30. *New-York Journal, and General Advertiser*, 24 Mar. 1785.

31. *The New-York Daily Gazette*, 3 Feb. 1791. See also Ibid., 12, 22 Feb. 1791.

32. *Daily Advertiser*, 10 April 1792.

33. *Pennsylvania Packet, and Daily Advertiser*, 25 Sept. 1786.

34. Ibid., 26 Sept. 1786.

35. Ibid., 27 Sept. 1786.
36. *Maryland Journal and Baltimore Advertiser*, 12 Sept. 1794. See also Ibid., 14 Feb. 1794.
37. Ibid., 12 Sept. 1794. See also Ibid., 14 Feb., 3 Mar. 1794.
38. Ibid., 12 Sept. 1794.
39. *Aurora General Advertiser*, 1 Feb. 1796.
40. *Columbian Centinel*, 4 Feb. 1792.
41. Mitchell and Flanders, *Statutes of Pennsylvania*, 13:195-214.
42. Carey and Bioren, *Laws of Pennsylvania*, 5:196-98.
43. Sidney I. Pomerantz, *New York, an American City, 1783-1803* (New York, 1938), pp. 54-56.
44. *Laws and Ordinances of the City of Albany* (Albany, 1808), pp. 137-40.
45. B. Drake and E. D. Mansfield, *Cincinnati in 1826* (Cincinnati, 1827), pp. 50-51.
46. Kilty, *Laws of Maryland*, vol. 2 (1796), chap. 96.
47. Howard L. McBain, "The Evolution of Types of City Government in the United States," *National Municipal Review*, 6 (Jan. 1917): 19-30; John Wooldridge, ed., *History of Nashville, Tennessee* (Nashville, Tenn., 1890), p. 112.
48. Pomerantz, *New York, an American City*, p. 134.
49. James Cheetham, *Annals of the Corporation* (New York, 1802), p. 7.
50. Munsell, *Annals of Albany*, 6:126; 7:140.
51. Ibid., 8:174.
52. The number of candidates vying for Albany's twenty council seats was as follows: 1828, 38; 1829, 34; 1830, 37; 1831, 40; 1832, 39; 1833, 40. Ibid., pp. 174, 192, 217, 232, 256, 273. For further information about the general development of party rivalry in the United States see Richard Hofstadter, *The Idea of a Party System: The Rise of Legitimate Opposition in the United States, 1780-1840* (Berkeley, 1969); William N. Chambers, *Political Parties in a New Nation: The American Experience, 1776-1809* (New York, 1963); and Richard P. McCormick, *The Second American Party System: Party Formation in the Jacksonian Era* (Chapel Hill, 1966). Partisan divisions on the municipal level did not arise from conflict over municipal issues but instead reflected the divisions on the state and national levels. The development of party rivalry on the municipal level thus conforms to the pattern of party development on the state and national level as described by these authors.
53. Griffith, *American City Government*, p. 199.
54. Mitchell and Flanders, *Statutes of Pennsylvania*, 15:463.
55. William Holcomb, "Pennsylvania Boroughs," *Johns Hopkins Studies in Historical and Political Science* 4 (1886): 165.

Chapter 6

1. *The Parliamentary Register; or, History of the Proceedings and Debates of the House of Commons* (London, 1784), 12:278, 376.
2. *Pennsylvania Packet, and Daily Advertiser*, 30 Aug., 25 Sept. 1786.
3. *Newport Mercury*, 14 Dec. 1786.

4. Ibid., 2 Oct. 1786.

5. Ibid., 14 May, 1787.

6. J. R. Bartlett, ed., *Records of the Colony of Rhode Island Providence Plantations in New England* (Providence, 1856–65), 10:233-34.

7. *Newport Herald*, 29 Mar. 1787.

8. Ibid., 22 Mar. 1787.

9. Information derived from "Norfolk Borough Council Minutes," Office of Norfolk City Clerk.

10. *Norfolk and Portsmouth Journal*, 12 Mar. 1788.

11. Ibid., 20 Feb. 1788.

12. "Norfolk Minutes," 15 Aug. 1786.

13. Ibid., 12 Oct. 1787.

14. Hening, *Virginia Statutes*, vol. 13.

15. "Norfolk Minutes," 28 May 1788.

16. Ibid., 28 May 1788.

17. *General Advertiser*, 17 Jan. 1792.

18. *Dunlap's American Daily Advertiser*, 19 Jan. 1792.

19. *General Advertiser*, 25 Jan. 1792.

20. Ibid., 17 Jan. 1792.

21. *Dunlap's American Daily Advertiser*, 19 Jan. 1792.

22. *General Advertiser*, 25 Jan. 1792.

23. Ibid., 17 Jan. 1792.

24. *Journal of the Senate of the Commonwealth of Pennsylvania, 1791–92* (Philadelphia, 1792), pp. 118-19.

25. *Independent Gazetteer; and Agricultural Repository*, 1 Dec. 1792.

26. A copy of one memorial urging reform is in the *Pennsylvania Gazette*, 30 Dec. 1795.

27. "Philadelphia Common Council Minutes," 9 Jan., 3 Mar. 1796, Philadelphia City Archives.

28. *Aurora General Advertiser*, 30 Jan. 1796.

29. Ibid.

30. Ibid., 6 Feb. 1796.

31. Mitchell and Flanders, *Statutes of Pennsylvania*, 15:462-64.

32. *Journal of the House of Assembly of the State of New-York* (New York, 1791), p. 13.

33. *New-York Journal and Patriotic Register*, 17 Feb. 1791.

34. Pomerantz, *New York, an American City*, p. 69.

35. *Daily Advertiser*, 10 Apr. 1792.

36. James Cheetham, *Annals of the Corporation, Relative to the Late Contested Election; with Strictures Upon the Conduct of the Majority* (New York, 1802), p. 77.

37. Ibid., p. 72.

38. Ibid., pp. 81-82.

39. Ibid., p. 86.

40. *New-York Evening Post*, 26 Mar. 1803.

41. *Morning Chronicle*, 23 Feb. 1803, as reprinted in "Burghers and Freemen," pp. 320-24.

42. Ibid., p. 299.

43. *New-York Evening Post,* 11 Apr. 1803.
44. *Morning Chronicle,* 19 Feb. 1803, as reprinted in "Burghers and Freemen," p. 319.
45. *New York Gazette and General Advertiser,* 10 Jan. 1803, as reprinted in "Burghers and Freemen," p. 305.
46. *New-York Evening Post,* 15, 18 Apr. 1803.
47. Street, *Council of Revision,* p. 425.
48. *Commercial Advertiser,* 29 Apr. 1803.
49. Ibid., 23 Apr. 1803.
50. *New-York Evening Post,* 12 Jan 1804, as reprinted in "Burghers and Freemen," p. 335.
51. "Burghers and Freemen," p. 324.
52. Street, *Council of Revision,* p. 328.
53. Wall, *Chronicles of New Brunswick,* p. 33.
54. *Dartmouth College* v. *Woodward* 4 Wheaton 518, 629–30.
55. 4 Wheaton 663.
56. 4 Wheaton 694.

Chapter 7

1. Talbot Hamlin, *Benjamin Latrobe* (New York, 1955), pp. 158–66; "Norfolk Council Orders," 25 Aug. 1800; *Minutes of the Common Council of the City of New York 1784–1831* (New York, 1917), 2:642, 645.
2. *Pennsylvania Packet; or, General Advertiser,* 2 Sept. 1783.
3. *Freeman's Journal; or, North American Intelligencer,* 8 Oct. 1781.
4. *Pennsylvania Packet, and Daily Advertiser,* 7 Aug. 1786; *Pennsylvania Herald, and General Advertiser,* 9 Aug. 1786.
5. *General Advertiser,* 17 Jan. 1792; *Dunlap's American Daily Advertiser,* 18 Jan. 1792.
6. *Dunlap's American Daily Advertiser,* 17 Jan. 1793.
7. *Independent Gazetteer, and Agricultural Repository,* 1 Dec. 1792.
8. *Maryland Journal and Baltimore Advertiser,* 12 Sept. 1794.
9. *New York Council Minutes,* 2:642, 645.
10. Ibid., 3:48–49, 53–55; *Commercial Advertiser,* 29 Oct. 1801.
11. *Commercial Advertiser,* 12 Nov. 1801.
12. Ibid., 13 Nov. 1801.
13. Ibid., 12 Nov. 1801.
14. Ibid., 13 Nov. 1801.
15. Ibid., 3, 4, 13 Nov., 9 Dec. 1801.
16. *New York Council Minutes,* 3:53–55; *Commercial Advertiser,* 20 Nov. 1801.
17. *New-York Evening Post,* 14 Mar. 1815. Reprinted in *Poulson's American Daily Advertiser,* 17 Mar. 1815.
18. *New-York Evening Post,* 16 Mar. 1815; *Poulson's American Daily Advertiser,* 20 Mar. 1815.
19. *New York Council Minutes,* 12:148.
20. *New-York Evening Post,* 30 Nov., 17 Dec. 1821.
21. *New-York Evening Post,* 31 Dec. 1821.

22. George Rogers Howell and Jonathan Tenney, *Bicentennial History of Albany and History of the County of Albany, N.Y., from 1609 to 1886* (New York, 1886), p. 470.

23. *Laws and Ordinances of the Common Council of the City of Albany, Revised and Revived, April 14, 1845* (Albany, 1845), pp. 12-14.

24. John C. Lowber and C. S. Miller, eds., *A Digest of the Ordinances of the Corporation of the City of Philadelphia; and of the Acts of Assembly Relating Thereto* (Philadelphia, 1822), p. 9; Carey and Bioren, *Laws of Pennsylvania*, 5:252-53; *Ordinances of the City of Baltimore* (Baltimore, 1807), pp. 39-40.

25. DeVoe,*Market Book*, pp. 210-11.

26. Ibid., p. 217.

27. Ibid., p. 227.

28. They were known as "shinners" in Philadelphia and "shirks" in New York City.

29. Scharf and Westcott, *Philadelphia*, 1:551.

30. Ibid., p. 582.

31. *New York Council Minutes*, 10:9.

32. DeVoe, *Market Book*, pp. 492-501; *New-York Evening Post*, 17, 18 Dec. 1821.

33. DeVoe, *Market Book*, p. 353.

34. Ibid., p. 382.

35. "Minutes of Philadelphia Common Council," Philadelphia City Archives, 11 Nov. 1819.

36. "Proceedings of Councils," *Hazard's Register of Pennsylvania* 3 (21 Mar. 1829): 184-85.

37. Timothy Dwight, *Travels in New England and New York* (Cambridge, Mass., 1969), 1:139.

38. James Kent, *The Charter of the City of New-York, With Notes Thereon* (New York, 1836), p. 148.

39. *Pennsylvania Gazette*, 18 Oct. 1764.

40. W. P. Holcomb, "Pennsylvania Boroughs," *Johns Hopkins Studies in Historical and Political Science* 4:169; Arthur C. Binning, "The Iron Plantations of Early Pennsylvania," *Pennsylvania Magazine of History and Biography* 57 (1933): 129; Dorian Green, *A History of Bristol Borough* (Camden, N.J., 1911), p. 69.

41. *Minutes of the Council of Philadelphia 1704 to 1776*, p. 803.

42. Holcomb, "Pennsylvania Boroughs," p. 169; Binning, "Iron Plantations," p. 129; Green, *Bristol*, p. 69.

43. J. H. Powell, *Bring out Your Dead: The Great Plague of Yellow Fever in Philadelphia in 1793* (Philadelphia, 1949), p. 282; B. W. Kunkel, *Milestones to Health in Pennsylvania: A History of Public Health Work in the State* (n.p., n.d.), p. 21.

44. J. Thomas Scharf, *History of Delaware 1609-1888* (Philadelphia, 1888), vol. 2; Edward E. Atwater, ed., *History of the City of New Haven, Connecticut* (New York, 1887), 2:448; Thomas Gamble, Jr., *A History of the City Government of Savannah, Georgia, From 1790 to 1901* (Savannah, 1900), p. 82.

45. Carey and Bioren, *Laws of Pennsylvania*, 4:390-412; Pomerantz, *New York, an American City*, p. 343.

46. *New York Council Minutes,* 2:500-507.

47. Edward E. Atwater, ed., *History of the City of New Haven, Connecticut* (New York, 1887), 2:448.

48. Kunkel, *Milestones to Health in Pennsylvania,* p. 22.

49. George B. Eckhard, ed., *A Digest of the Ordinances of the City Council of Charleston From the Year 1783 to Oct. 1844* (Charleston, S.C., 1844), p. 257.

50. *Laws of Albany,* p. 40.

51. *Ordinances of Norfolk,* p. 153.

52. *New York Council Minutes,* 4:203-4.

53. *New York Council Minutes,* 2:100-101, 202; Carey and Bioren, *Laws of Pennsylvania,* 4:410.

54. *Ordinances of Baltimore,* p. 110; Eckhard, *Digest of the Ordinances of Charleston,* pp. 122-23. For the municipality's role in the founding of a hospital in Savannah, Georgia, see Gamble, *City Government of Savannah,* p. 82.

55. "Petitions to the Councils of Philadelphia," Historical Society of Pennsylvania, 22 Jan. 1801.

56. Ibid., 9 Dec. 1802.

57. Ibid., 2 Feb. 1802.

58. Adolph B. Benson, ed., *Peter Kalm's Travels in North America* (New York, 1937), 1:133, 339.

59. Munsell, *Collections on the History of Albany,* 1:119.

60. Charles King, *A Memoir of the Construction, Cost, and Capacity of the Croton Aqueduct, Compiled from Official Documents* (New York, 1843), pp. 85-88; Edwards and Peterson, *New York as an Eighteenth Century Municipality,* pp. 339-41; Lancaster Borough Minutes, Lancaster City Clerk's Office, 14 Sept. 1772.

61. "Minutes of Philadelphia City Council," 1 Aug. 1799.

62. *Philadelphia Gazette,* 31 July 1800.

63. For an account of the proposals concerning water before the 1830s see King, *Croton Aqueduct.*

64. *New York Council Minutes,* p. 507.

65. Atwater, *History of New Haven,,* 2:448.

66. Scharf, *History of Delaware,* 2:665.

67. "Lancaster City Minutes," Lancaster City Clerk's Office, 4 Jan. 1831, 1 Feb. 1831; Wooldridge, *History of Nashville,* pp. 130-33.

68. *Daily Advertiser,* 3 Apr. 1802; Pomerantz, *New York, an American City,* pp. 286-88.

69. *New York Council Minutes,* 3:434.

70. Ibid., 4:175.

71. Scharf and Westcott, *Philadelphia,* 3:1845-46.

72. Gamble, *City Government of Savannah,* pp. 83-84, 123.

73. Eckhard, *Digest of the Ordinances of Charleston,* p. 290.

74. *Ordinances of Baltimore,* p. 143; *Laws of Albany,* p. 22.

75. *Laws and Ordinances Ordained and Established by the Mayor, Aldermen, and Commonalty of the City of New-York* (New York, 1817), p. 118.

76. Pomerantz, *New York, an American City,* p. 250; Lowber and Miller, *Ordinances of Philadelphia,* pp. 35-38; Allinson and Penrose, *Philadelphia,* p. 74.

77. *New York Council Minutes*, 8:783-85; Scharf and Westcott, *Philadelphia*, 1:583.

78. "Records of the Borough of Pittsburgh," Historical Society of Pennsylvania, 31 July 1802.

79. One notable exception to this rule was Philadelphia's charter of 1789. Within a year of its grant, however, the Pennsylvania legislature had enacted a law giving the corporation the authority to levy property or poll taxes.

80. David J. McCord, ed., *The Statutes at Large of South Carolina* (Columbia, S.C., 1840), p. 98.

81. *The Public Statute Laws of the State of Connecticut* (Hartford, 1808) 1:134-35. For the broad powers of taxation granted to other Connecticut cities see *Statute Laws of Connecticut*, 1:143, 153-54, 166, 176.

82. Kilty, *Laws of Maryland*, vol. 2, chap. 96.

83. Pomerantz, *New York, an American City*, pp. 356-63.

Chapter 8

1. DeVoe, *Market Book*, p. 382.

2. Milo Roy Maltbie, "Municipal Functions: A Study of the Development, Scope and Tendency of Municipal Socialism," *Municipal Affairs* 2 (Dec. 1898): 676.

3. See, for example, Frederick S. Lamb, "Municipal Art," *Municipal Affairs* 1 (Dec. 1897): 674-88; Karl Bitter, "Municipal Sculpture," *Municipal Affairs* 2 (Mar. 1898): 73-97; Edwin Howland Blashfield, "A Word for Municipal Art," *Municipal Affairs* 3 (Dec. 1899): 582-93.

Bibliography

Municipal and Town Records

Manuscript

"Lancaster City Minutes." Office of City Clerk, Lancaster, Pennsylvania.

"Lancaster, Pennsylvania, Minutes of the Borough of." Office of the City Clerk, Lancaster, Pennsylvania.

"Norfolk Borough Council Orders." Office of City Clerk, Norfolk, Virginia.

"Philadelphia Common Council Minutes." Philadelphia City Archives.

"Philadelphia, Petitions to the Councils of." Historical Society of Pennsylvania, Philadelphia, Pennsylvania.

"Pittsburgh, Records of the Borough of." Historical Society of Pennsylvania, Philadelphia, Pennsylvania.

Printed—Great Britain

Bateson, Mary, et al., eds. *Records of the Borough of Leicester.* 6 vols. Cambridge and Leicester, 1899–1967.

Chandler, George. *Liverpool under James I.* Liverpool, 1960.

Cox, J. Charles. *The Records of the Borough of Northampton.* 2 vols. London, 1898.

Dennett, J., ed. *Beverley Borough Records, 1575–1821.* Wakefield, U.K., 1933.

Exeter, Report on the Records of the City of. London, 1916.

Fripp, Edgar I., ed. *Minutes and Accounts of the Corporation of Stratford-upon-Avon and Other Records 1553–1620.* 4 vols. Oxford, 1921–30.

NOTE: Titles of municipal records and statutes have been inverted and alphabetized by town.

Gibbs, A. E., ed. *The Corporation Records of St. Albans.* Saint Albans, U.K., 1890.

Guilding, J. M., ed. *Reading Records, Diary of the Corporation.* 4 vols. London and Oxford, 1892-96.

Pape, T. *Newcastle-under-Lyme in Tudor and Early Stuart Times,* Manchester, 1938.

Raine, Angelo, ed. *York Civic Records.* 8 vols. York, 1939–53.

Rutledge, P., ed. "Great Yarmouth Assembly Minutes, 1538–1545," *Norfolk Record Society* 39 (1970): 5–80.

Sachse, William L., ed. *Minutes of the Norwich Court of Mayoralty, 1630-1831.* Norwich, 1942.

Stevenson, W. H., et al. *Records of the Borough of Nottingham.* 6 vols. London, 1882–1914.

Turner, William H., ed. *Selections from the Records of the City of Oxford.* Oxford, 1880.

Printed—United States

Baltimore Town and Jones Town 1729–1797, First Records of. Baltimore, 1905.

Boston Town Records, Boston Record Commissioners Reports. 29 vols. Boston, 1880–1902.

"The Burghers of New Amsterdam and the Freemen of New York, 1675–1866," *Collections of the New-York Historical Society For the Year 1885,* vol. 18.

The Charter of the City of New Brunswick of December 30, 1730 and Early Ordinances of the City. New Brunswick, 1913.

Fernow, Berthold, ed. *The Records of New Amsterdam From 1653 to 1674 Anno Domini.* 7 vols. New York, 1897.

"Ledger Number I, Chamberlain's Office, Corporation of the City of New York." *Collections of the New-York Historical Society* 42 (1909): 1–110.

Morris, Richard B., ed. *Select Cases of the Mayor's Court of New York City, 1674-1784.* Washington, D.C., 1935.

Munsell, Joel, ed. *The Annals of Albany.* 10 vols. Albany, 1854–59.

———. *Collections on the History of Albany.* 4 vols. Albany, 1865–71.

New York, 1675–1776, Minutes of the Common Council of the City of. 9 vols. New York, 1905.

New York, 1784–1831, Minutes of the Common Council of the City of. 21 vols. New York, 1917,

1930.

Philadelphia 1704 to 1776, Minutes of the Common Council of the City of. Philadelphia, 1847.

Statutes and Ordinances

Albany, Laws and Ordinances of the City of. Albany 1808.

Albany, Laws and Ordinances of the Mayor, Recorder, Aldermen, and Commonalty of the City of. Albany, 1773.

Albany, Revised and Revived, April 14, 1845, Laws and Ordinances of the Common Council of the City of. Albany, 1845.

Annapolis in Maryland, The Bye-Laws of the City of. Annapolis, 1769.

Baltimore, Ordinances of the City of. Baltimore, 1807.

Boston, Several Rules, Orders, and By-Laws Made and Agreed Upon by the Freeholders and Inhabitants of. Boston, 1702.

Carey, M., and Bioren, J., eds. *Laws of the Commonwealth of Pennsylvania 1700–1802.* 6 vols. Philadelphia, 1803.

Clark, Walter, ed. *The State Records of North Carolina 1777–1790.* 16 vols. Winston and Goldsboro, 1895–1905.

Connecticut, The Public Statute Laws of the State of. Hartford, 1808.

Eckhard, George B., ed. *A Digest of the Ordinances of the City Council of Charleston From the Year 1783 to Oct. 1844.* Charleston, 1844.

Edwards, Alexander, ed. *Ordinances of the City Council of Charleston . . . Passed Since the Incorporation of the City.* Charleston, 1807.

Hening, William W., ed. *The Statutes at Large; Being A Collection of all the Laws of Virginia, From the First Session of the Legislature, in the Year 1619.* 13 vols. Richmond, 1810–23.

Kilty, William, ed. *Laws of Maryland.* 2 vols. Annapolis, 1799–1800.

Lowber, John C., and Miller, C. S., eds. *A Digest of the Corporation of the City of Philadelphia; and of the Acts of Assembly Relating Thereto.* Philadelphia, 1822.

McCord, David J., and Cooper, Thomas, eds. *The*

Statutes at Large of South Carolina. 9 vols. Columbia, S.C., 1836–41.

Massachusetts Bay, Acts and Resolves of the Province of the. 5 vols. Boston, 1869–86.

Mitchell, J. T., and Flanders, Henry, comps. *The Statutes at Large of Pennsylvania From 1682 to 1801.* 16 vols. Harrisburg, Pa., 1911.

New Haven in Connecticut, Bye Laws of the City of. New Haven, 1803.

New Jersey, Statutes of. Trenton, 1804.

New London, Connecticut By-Laws. New London, 1805.

New York, The Colonial Laws of. 5 vols. Albany, 1894.

New-York City, Ordinances Enacted by the Mayor and Common Council of. New York, 1805.

New-York, Laws, Statutes, Ordinances and Constitutions, Ordained, Made, and Established by the Mayor, Aldermen and Commonalty of the City of. New York, 1774.

New-York . . . , Several Laws, Orders & Ordinances Established by the Mayor, Recorder, Aldermen and Assistants of the City of. New York, 1707.

Norfolk, The Ordinances of. Norfolk, 1829.

Philadelphia, Ordinances and Laws Relating to. Philadelphia, 1805.

Shurtleff, Nathaniel, ed. *Records of the Governor and Company of the Massachusetts Bay in New England.* 5 vols. Boston, 1853–54.

Pamphlets and Broadsides

At a Meeting of the Freeholders and Other Inhabitants of the Town of Boston. . . . Boston, 1734.

Cheetham, James. *Annals of the Corporation, Relative to the Late Contested Election; with Strictures Upon the Conduct of the Majority.* New York, 1802.

Colman, Benjamin. *Some Reasons and Arguments Offered to the Good People of Boston and Adjacent Places for the Setting Up Markets in Boston.* Boston, 1719.

Ford, Worthington Chauncey, ed. "Communication of Two Documents Protesting Against the Incorporation of Boston." *Publications of the Colonial Society of Massachusetts,* 10 (1904–6): 345–52.

Goddard, William. *Andrew Marvell's Second Address to the Inhabitants of Philadelphia.* Philadelphia, 1773.

———. *To My Fellow Citizens, Friends to Liberty, and Enemies to Despotism.* Philadelphia, 1773.

Seasonable Reflections on Dissolving Corporations, In the Late Two Reigns, by Surrendering of, and Giving Judgment Against Charters. ... London, 1689.

To the Freemen, Citizens of Philadelphia. No. 1. Philadelphia, 1773.

To the Freemen, Citizens of Philadelphia. No. 2. Philadelphia, 1773.

Newspapers

Annapolis, Maryland
   Maryland Gazette
Baltimore, Maryland
   The Maryland Journal and Baltimore Advertiser
Boston, Massachusetts
   American Herald
   Boston Evening Post
   The Boston Gazette and the Country Journal
   Columbian Centinel
   The Massachusetts Centinel: and the Republican Journal
Newport, Rhode Island
   The Newport Herald
   The Newport Mercury
New York City, New York
   Commercial Advertiser
   The Daily Advertiser
   Klein, Milton, ed. *The Independent Reflector; or, Weekly Essays on Sundry Important Subjects.* Cambridge, Mass., 1968
   Morning Chronicle
   The New-York Daily Gazette
   New-York Evening Post
   New York Gazette
   The New York Gazette and General Advertiser
   The New York Gazette Revived in the Weekly Post Boy
   The New York Journal & Patriotic Register
   The New-York Journal, and the General Advertiser
   New York Mercury

New-York Weekly Journal
New York Weekly Post Boy
Norfolk, Virginia
  The Norfolk and Portsmouth Journal
Philadelphia, Pennsylvania
  Aurora General Advertiser
  Dunlap's American Daily Advertiser
  The Freeman's Journal; or, the North American Intelligencer
  General Advertiser
  The Independent Gazetteer, and Agricultural Repository
  Pennsylvania Gazette
  The Pennsylvania Herald, and General Advertiser
  The Pennsylvania Packet; or, the General Advertiser
  Philadelphia Gazette
  Poulson's American Daily Advertiser

Local Studies and Sources

Allinson, Edward P., and Penrose, Boies. *Philadelphia, 1681–1887*. Baltimore, 1887.

———. eds. "The Early Government of Philadelphia, and the Blue Anchor Tavern Landing." *Pennsylvania Magazine of History and Biography* 10 (1886): 61-77.

Ashford, L. J. *The History of the Borough of High Wycombe from Its Origins to 1880*. London, 1960.

Atkinson, Tom. *Elizabethan Winchester*. London, 1963.

Atwater, Edward E., ed. *History of the City of New Haven, Connecticut*. 2 vols. New York, 1887.

Bartlett, J. R., ed. *Records of the Colony of Rhode Island and Providence Plantations in New England*. 10 vols. Providence, 1856–65.

Benedict, William H. *New Brunswick in History*. New Brunswick, 1925.

Binning, Arthur C. "The Iron Plantations of Early Pennsylvania." *Pennsylvania Magazine of History and Biography*, 57 (1933): 117-37.

Boyle, J. R., ed. *Charters and Letters Patent Granted to Kingston upon Hull*. Hull, 1905.

Brown, Henry Collins, ed. *Valentine's Manual of Old New York, 1925*. New York, 1924.

"The Building of Williamsburg." *William and Mary Quarterly Historical Magazine*, 1st ser., 10 (Oct.

1901): 73–98.

DeVoe, Thomas. *The Market Book: A History of the Public Markets of the City of New York*. New York, 1862.

Diamondstone, Judith. "The Philadelphia Corporation, 1701–1776." Ph.D. diss., University of Pennsylvania, 1969.

―――. "Philadelphia's Municipal Corporation, 1701–1776." *Pennsylvania Magazine of History and Biography*, 90 (Apr. 1966): 183–201.

Drake, B., and Mansfield, E. D. *Cincinnati in 1826*. Cincinnati, 1827.

Dutcher, Salem, and Jones, Charles C. *Memorial History of Augusta, Georgia*. Syracuse, 1890.

Edwards, George. "New York City Politics before the American Revolution." *Political Science Quarterly* 36 (Dec. 1921): 586–602.

Edwards, George, and Peterson, Arthur. *New York as an Eighteenth Century Municipality*. New York, 1917.

Egle, William Henry, ed. *Pennsylvania Archives, Third Series*, vol. 14. Harrisburg, 1897.

Ellis, Franklin, and Evans, Samuel. *History of Lancaster County, Pennsylvania*. Philadelphia, 1883.

Felt, Joseph B. "Ancient Application of Boston For A City Charter." *New England Historical and Genealogical Register* 11 (July 1857): 206–10.

Gamble, Thomas, Jr., ed. *A History of the City Government of Savannah, Georgia, From 1790 to 1901*. Savannah, 1900.

Green, Dorian. *A History of Bristol Borough*. Camden, N.J., 1911.

Hatfield, Edwin F. *History of Elizabeth, New Jersey*. New York, 1868.

Herbert, William. *The History of the Twelve Great Livery Companies of London*. 2 vols. London, 1834.

Hilkey, Charles J. "Legal Development in Colonial Massachusetts." *Studies in History, Economics, and Public Law*, 37 (1910): 29–50.

Hill, J. W. F. *Georgian Lincoln*. Cambridge, 1966.

―――. *Tudor and Stuart Lincoln*. Cambridge, 1956.

Hislop, Codman. *Albany: Dutch, English, and American*. Albany, 1936.

Holcomb, W. P., "Pennsylvania Boroughs." *Johns*

Hopkins Studies in Historical and Political Science 4 (1886): 129–79.

Howell, George Rogers, and Tenney, Jonathan. *Bicentennial History of Albany and History of the County of Albany, N.Y., from 1609 to 1886.* New York, 1886.

Kent, James. *The Charter of the City of New-York, With Notes Thereon.* New York, 1836.

King, Charles. *A Memoir of the Construction, Cost, and Capacity of the Croton Aqueduct, Compiled from Official Documents.* New York, 1843.

Kunkel, B. W. *Milestones to Health in Pennsylvania: A History of Public Health Work in the State.* N.p., n.d.

Levin, Jennifer. *The Charter Controversy in the City of London, 1660–1688, and Its Consequences.* London, 1969.

Limpus, Lowell. *History of the New York Fire Department.* New York, 1940.

Lockridge, Kenneth A. *A New England Town: The First Hundred Years.* New York, 1970.

McAnear, Beverly. "The Place of the Freeman in Old New York." *New York History* 21 (Oct. 1940): 418–30.

Maitland, Frederic W., and Bateson, Mary, eds. *The Charters of the Borough of Cambridge.* Cambridge, 1901.

Maitland, William. *The History and Survey of London From Its Foundation to the Present Time.* London, 1756.

Matthews, Albert. "Remarks on Attempts to Incorporate Boston." *Publications of the Colonial Society of Boston* 10 (1904–6): 352–56.

Murray, Nicholas. *Notes, Historical and Biographical, Concerning Elizabeth-town, Its Eminent Men, Churches and Ministers.* Elizabeth, 1844.

"New-York Tax Lists 1695–1699." *Collections of the New-York Historical Society for the Year 1911,* vol. 44.

"Notes and Queries." *New York Genealogical and Biographical Record* 20 (Jan. 1889): 42–43.

Patterson, A. Temple. *A History of Southampton, 1700–1914.* 2 vols. Southampton, 1966–71.

Pearson, Jonathan, et al. *A History of the Sche-*

nectady Patent in Dutch and English Times.
Albany, 1883.

*Pennsylvania, 1791–92, Journal of the Senate of the
Commonwealth of.* Philadelphia, 1792.

Pomerantz, Sidney I. *New York, an American City,
1783–1803.* New York, 1938.

Powell, J. H. *Bring out Your Dead: The Great
Plague of Yellow Fever in Philadelphia in 1793.*
Philadelphia, 1949.

Powell, Mary G. *The History of Old Alexandria,
Virginia.* Richmond, 1928.

"Proceedings of Councils." *Hazard's Register of
Pennsylvania* 3 (21 Mar. 1829): 184–85.

Quinn, Silvanus Jackson. *The History of the City of
Fredericksburg, Virginia.* Richmond, 1908.

Ridgeley, David, ed. *Annals of Annapolis, Comprising Sundry Notices of That Old City.* Baltimore, 1841.

Riley, Elihu S. *The Ancient City: A History of
Annapolis, in Maryland.* Annapolis, 1887.

Rutman, Darrett B. *Winthrop's Boston, Portrait of a
Puritan Town 1630–1649.* Chapel Hill, 1965.

Scharf, J. Thomas. *History of Delaware 1609–1888.*
2 vols. Philadelphia, 1888.

Scharf, J. Thomas, and Westcott, Thompson. *History of Philadelphia, 1609–1884.* 3 vols. Philadelphia, 1884.

Scott, Austin. "The Early Cities of New Jersey."
Proceedings of the New Jersey Historical Society,
2d ser., 9 (1886–87): 151–73.

Sewall, Samuel. *The History of Woburn.* Boston,
1868.

Street, Alfred B., ed. *The Council of Revision of the
State of New York.* Albany, 1859.

Trelease, Allen W. *Indian Affairs in Colonial New
York: The Seventeenth Century.* Ithaca, N.Y.,
1960.

Valentine, David T., ed. *Manual of the Common
Council of New York for 1860.* New York, 1859.

Wall, John P. *The Chronicles of New Brunswick,
New Jersey 1667–1931.* New Brunswick, 1931.

Warden, G. B. *Boston 1689-1776.* Boston, 1970.

Willcox, William B. *Gloucestershire, a Study in Local
Government, 1590–1640.* New Haven, 1940.

Wilson, James Grant, ed. *The Memorial History of the City of New-York*. 4 vols. New York, 1892–93.

Wooldridge, John, ed. *History of Nashville, Tennessee*. Nashville, 1890.

Other Sources

Benson, Adolph B., ed. *Peter Kalm's Travels in North America*. 2 vols. New York, 1937.

Bitter, Karl. "Municipal Sculpture." *Municipal Affairs* 2 (Mar. 1898): 73–97.

Blashfield, Edwin Howland. "A Word for Municipal Art." *Municipal Affairs* 3 (Dec. 1899): 582–93.

Bridenbaugh, Carl. *The Colonial Craftsmen*. New York, 1950.

———. *Cities in the Wilderness*. New York, 1938.

Cheyney, Edward. *A History of England from the Defeat of the Armada to the Death of Elizabeth*. New York, 1948.

Douglas, Paul H. *American Apprenticeship and Industrial Education*. New York, 1921.

Dwight, Timothy. *Travels in New England and New York*. 4 vols. Cambridge, Mass., 1969.

Fairlie, John A. "Municipal Corporations in the Colonies." *Municipal Affairs* 2 (Sept. 1898): 341–81.

Ford, Paul L., ed. *The Writings of Thomas Jefferson*. 10 vols. New York, 1892–99.

Greene, Evarts B., and Harrington, Virginia D. *American Population before the Federal Census of 1790*. New York, 1932.

Griffith, Ernest S. *History of American City Government: The Colonial Period*. New York, 1938.

Hamlin, Talbot. *Benjamin Henry Latrobe*. New York, 1955.

Jarrett, Derek. *Britain 1688–1815*. London, 1965.

Keys, Alice M. *Cadwallader Colden: A Representative Eighteenth Century Official*. New York, 1906.

Lamb, Frederick S. "Municipal Art." *Municipal Affairs* 1 (Dec. 1897): 674–88.

Land, Aubrey C. *The Dulanys of Maryland*. Baltimore, 1955.

Lecky, William E. H. *A History of England in the Eighteenth Century*. 8 vols. New York, 1883.

McBain, Howard L. "The Evolution of Types of

City Government in the United States." *National Municipal Review* 6 (Jan. 1917): 19–30.

McKee, Samuel, Jr. *Labor in Colonial New York, 1664–1776.* New York, 1935.

MacLear, Anne Bush. "Early New England Towns: A Comparative Study of Their Development." *Studies in History, Economics and Public Law* 29 (1908): 55–80.

Maltbie, Milo Roy. "Municipal Functions: A Study of the Development, Scope and Tendency of Municipal Socialism." *Municipal Affairs* 2 (Dec. 1898): 577–799.

Morris, Richard B. *Government and Labor in Early America.* New York, 1946.

The Parliamentary Register; or, History of the Proceedings and Debates of the House of Commons. Vol. 12. London, 1784.

Smellie, K. B. *Great Britain since 1688: A Modern History.* Ann Arbor, 1962.

Smith, Adam. *An Inquiry into the Nature and Causes of the Wealth of Nations.* 2d ed. London, 1778.

Spencer, Frederick H. *Municipal Origins.* London, 1911.

Stubbs, S. G. Blaxland, and Bligh, E. W. *Sixty Centuries of Health and Physick.* London, 1931.

Webb, Sidney, and Webb, Beatrice. *English Local Government from the Revolution to the Municipal Corporations Act: The Manor and the Borough.* 2 vols. London, 1908.

———. *Statutory Authorities for Special Purposes.* London, 1922.

Index

Adams, Samuel, 67
Albany: charter, 119; content distribution of ordinances, 18, 52, 109–10; county authority, 34; elections, 77; fire protection, 53; forestalling and engrossing, 23–24; freeman status, 19, 49; health measures, 54, 103; judicial authority, 27; municipal officials, 26, 61, 128; parks and landscaping, 107; party rivalry, 76–77; price regulation, 22, 51, 97; quality regulation, 24; revenues and taxation, 28–29, 55; royal authority, 33–34; separation of powers, 74; street lighting, 55; suffrage requirements, 30; vocational restrictions, 20, 21–22, 50; water supply, 104–5
Aldeburgh, U.K., 117
Alexandria, Virginia, 58, 66–67, 129
Allen, Nehemiah, 26
Allen, William, 56–57
Annapolis, Maryland: charter, 17, 119; county authority, 34; elections, 29, 32–33; fire protection, 53; forestalling and engrossing, 23; health measures, 54; judicial authority, 27; revenues and taxation, 28; suffrage requirements, 30
Anti-Constitutionalists, Pennsylvania, 67, 82, 83, 85
Augusta, Georgia, 129

Badcock, Henry, 26
Baltimore, Maryland: commission government, 58; health measures, 103; parks and landscaping, 107; price regulation, 94, 96; revenues and taxation, 108; separation of powers, 69, 75; suffrage requirements, 72–73; tenure of officials, 73; weights and measures, 97
Berwick-upon-Tweed, 5, 117
Beverley, U.K.: content distribution of ordinances and orders, 12; forestalling and engrossing, 10; price regulation, 9; quality regulation, 10; vocational restrictions, 9
Bleecker, John, 61
Bossiney, U.K., 117
Boston, Massachusetts: annual elections, 73; charter proposals, 37–39; content distribution of by-laws, 36; county authority, 36–37, 125; criticism of economic restrictions, 38, 40–41; defense of town meeting government, 41–42, 70–71; provincial authority, 36–37; public markets, 39–40, 42–43, 124; revenues and taxation, 36; separation of powers, 69–70
Bristol, Pennsylvania: admission to council meetings, 78; charter, 17, 119, 123; elections, 30; fairs, 101
Bristol, U.K., 15
Burlington, New Jersey: charters, 120, 129; fairs, 101; price regulation, 22; royal authority, 124
Burrites, 77

Calvert, Cornelius and John, 81
Carlisle, Pennsylvania, 66
Carmalthen, U.K., 117
Charleston, South Carolina: content distribution of ordinances, 109; health measures, 103; parks and landscaping, 107; price regulation, 95; revenues and taxation, 108;